British Di

The 1960s

Volume Two

Marianne Faithfull

Sandie Shaw

Lulu

David Bret

Copyright David Bret 2017

David Bret has asserted his moral right to be identified as the Author of this Work in accordance with the Copyright Designs and Patents Act 1988. All rights reserved. No part of this publication may be reproduced or transmitted in any form or by any means, electronic or mechanical, including photocopying, recording or any information storage or retrieval system without the permission in writing from David Bret.

A catalogue record for this book is available from the British Library.

ISBN: 978-1543269246

*N'oublie pas....La vie sans amis c'est
Comme un jardin sans fleurs*

Acknowledgements

Writing this book would not have been possible had it not been for the inspiration, criticisms and love of that select group of individuals who, whether they be in this world or the next, I will always regard as my true family and *autre coeur*: Barbara, Irene Bevan, Marlene Dietrich, René Chevalier, Axel Dotti, Dorothy Squires, Anne Taylor and Roger Normand, Lucette Chevalier, David Bolt, *que vous dormez en paix*; Jacqueline Danno, Hélène Delavault, Betty and Gérard Gamain, Annick Roux, John Taylor, Terry Sanderson, Charley Marouani. Also a very special mention for Amália Rodrigues, Peter Burton, Joey Stefano, those *hiboux, fadistas* and *amis de foutre* who happened along the way, and *mes enfants perdus*. Thanks too to my agent wife, Jeanne, for putting up with my bad moods and for still being the keeper of my soul. And finally a *grand chapeau bas* to Marianne, Sandie and Lulu for the beautiful music!

N'oublie pas....La vie sans amis c'est
Comme un jardin sans fleurs

Marianne Faithfull

Unlike the other Brit Girls, who were partially adapted to the mechanics of the music industry before hitting the big time, Marianne Faithfull had no time to prepare for a career when, virtually overnight, she was catapulted into the spotlight. The daughter of a British wartime spy and an Austro-Hungarian baroness, she epitomized the perfect English rose—immaculate bone structure, long flowing blonde hair, angelic features, and an exquisite cut-glass accent. Yet when one harks back to this period in her life, Marianne is remembered far less for the beautiful songs she performed than she is for infiltrating the Rolling Stones' court and becoming consort to the Prince of Pop himself, Mick Jagger.

Marianne's memoirs, published in 1994, leave absolutely no stone unturned: she discusses with unflinching frankness the years of hedonism, and a fall from grace which would have finished off most mortals—heroin addiction, a suicide attempt, ill health which persists to this day, unsavoury and certainly undeserved headlines.

Yet in the face of even the harshest adversity, whether self-inflicted or the victim of circumstance, Marianne dragged herself out of the mire to become one of the most respected, adored and profoundly talented entertainers ever to have graced the world stage. From pop and folk to *sprechsinger*, from rock chick to *chanteuse-réaliste*, Marianne Faithfull has survived longer than any contemporary. She has absolutely no equal, and may well be the finest and most distinguished female vocalist in Britain today.

1: Oh, Look Around You

She was born Marian Evelyn Faithfull on 29 December 1946 at a Hampstead clinic, into a distinguished but undeniably eccentric family. Her father was Major Robert Glynn Faithfull—always known as Glynn—a former British intelligence officer and at the time of his daughter's birth an eminent professor of psychology. Her mother was Eva von Sacher-Masoch: Baroness Erisso—a title which Marianne subsequently inherited, but never used. Eva, of Jewish lineage on her mother's side and a descendent of the Hapsburg dynasty, was born in Budapest in 1912, the same year as Glynn. Formerly a student ballerina with the Max Reinhardt Company, Eva appeared in several Brecht and Weill productions—a tradition which her daughter continued years later. Eva's great uncle was Leopold von Sacher Masoch, who in 1870 published the controversial erotic novel, *Venus Im Pelz* (Venus In Furs) which added a new word to the dictionary—*masochist*.

Glynn and Eva met in Vienna towards the end of World War II. The city had been recently liberated by the Russians, one of whose soldiers had raped Eva, resulting in her having an abortion. Marianne later said that the soldier also attempted to rape her grandmother, and would have done if Eva had not pulled a gun, and shot him dead. How Eva managed to get away with the killing is not known. At the time she was working as a magazine editor and residing at the Hungarian Institute with her parents, Flora and Artur, while Glynn was heavily involved in espionage activities, his latest mission, delivering a secret message to Eva's brother, Alexander, working for Tito's partisans in Yugoslavia. Of equal importance, Glynn is thought to have been one of the team responsible for interrogating Heinrich Himmler, the head of Hitler's SS responsible for the murders of millions of Jews in extermination and concentration camps. This evil man evaded the rope by swallowing a cyanide capsule. Marianne later said that if her father had got Himmler to the Nuremberg Trials, he would have been given a knighthood, and that this would have changed the entire course of his life.

Eva had been looking to leave Europe for some time, and Glynn provided her with the perfect opportunity to do so. The couple, both the same age, appear to have fallen in love on impulse. They married in the autumn of 1945, and soon afterwards relocated to Liverpool, where Glynn accepted a post at the University. Almost at once the rot set in. "Had they seen each other's true natures, they would not have stayed together for one day," Marianne recalled, adding they had nothing in common—for whereas Eva had been extravagant and over-the-top theatrical, Glynn had been her "diametric opposite".

Upon learning that she was pregnant and on account of the acute housing shortage in those days, Eva temporarily moved to Hampstead to stay with Glynn's mother. It would take almost three years for the Faithfulls to reunite, when Glynn found them a semi-detached house in industrial Ormskirk, 13 miles north-east of the city. Here, in January 1952, Marianne, as she was already known, was enrolled at the local Church of England infant's school, and later at Christ Church School: the amendment of her name may have been in honour of the great French singer Marianne Oswald, a fellow Reinhardt student and Brecht and Weill *sprechsinger* whose "songs of soot and flame" she later performed. She remained an only child. Eva is known to have had three miscarriages, by which time her marriage to Glynn was all but over. They separated that same year, whence Eva and Marianne relocated to Reading, in Berkshire. Glynn, along with a friend who financed the project, moved into an 18th century manor house at Brazier's Park, Oxfordshire, where they set up a commune and institution for social research. Marianne, who described her father as "a truly obsessed eccentric, with utopian schemes for humanity and avant-garde theories of reform", was encouraged to visit and cynically recalled, "They appeared to be studying Dante and the Destiny of Man and all that, but what they were also doing was fucking like rabbits, with what were technically the *wrong* people." Whenever Eva showed up, she inevitably ended up having a row with one of the students—or Glynn—over the theories being taught, and eventually was banned from visiting altogether. The couple eventually divorced, and Glynn (though not Eva) married again and between 1963 and 1967 provided Marianne with two half-brothers and a half-sister.

Throughout her school years, Marianne lived with her mother (and during the first two years, Eva's mother, who had left Austria after her husband's death) in a small terraced house at 12 Milman Road, a run-down area just outside Reading's town centre—Marianne often referred to it as Reading Jail—after the infamous prison, where Oscar Wilde had been incarcerated, though her childhood seems to have been a fairly happy one. Away from school she took piano, singing and acting lessons, with a view to one day being accepted at RADA or, better still so far as her mother was concerned, at one of the Cambridge universities—Eva's expectations of her were high. Eva herself was regarded as a local curiosity. Ever the aristocrat she put on airs and graces, dressed differently than the other mothers, spoke English with a thick accent, and gossips were keen to know why her husband only visited every now and then, usually at the end of each university term. Eva also gave the impression of living beyond her means for someone employed as a shop assistant, then as a dance teacher with the town's Chiltern Nursery Training College. They gossiped about the "lodgers" she took in, deprived or abused teenagers she cared for like they might have been her own children. Some of these, along with Marianne, were given parts in the productions she staged at the Everyman Theatre, in London Road.

In some ways Eva resembled the mothers of Judy Garland and Maria Callas, in that whereas *she* had failed to make the grade in the entertainment world—not through lack of talent, but because circumstances had been against them—she wanted to ensure her daughter made the most of whatever talents she possessed. Eva also organised trips to London so that her daughter might experience the best that culture had to offer: premieres of the latest West End plays, classical music concerts, and a performance of *Il Trovatore* (and not *Tosca*, as Marianne erroneously states in her memoirs), with Maria Callas at Covent Garden.

9

In September 1953, Eva uprooted Marianne from Christ Church School and enrolled her at St Joseph's Convent, in Reading's Upper Redlands Road. Moreover, though the school was within walking distance of Milman Road, as the child of a "single-parent family" she was admitted as a charitable boarder and allowed home only on weekends. The stigma attached to this affected Marianne badly, as did the austere regime. Run by the Sisters of St Mary Magdalene, the pupils had it drilled into them, amongst other things, that nakedness was evil—therefore they were forced to bathe wearing full-length shifts. Not long after she transferred here, Marianne contracted tuberculosis—an episode of pyrrhic relief when she was confined to the front room at Milman Road for two months. Exactly why Eva had moved her non-Catholic daughter to a convent school is unclear, unless to thwart her father, who loathed the very concept of Catholicism. Puzzling too is why Marianne converted to the faith while there—she later said it had been "more by a Walter Pater aestheticism than veneration for the Pope." And any subject forbidden at school—art, adult literature, sex—was openly discussed at home. It was as if Eva was trying to teach her daughter how to become a rebel—and in the end, of course, inadvertently or not she succeeded.

Early in 1960, Marianne joined the Progress Theatre, a local self-supporting repertory group founded in 1946 and whose celebrated alumni later included Kenneth Branagh—the reason, she recalled, so that she would be able to act and meet boys. The 100-seater venue was home (and still is) to productions far removed from the usual "amateur dramatics musicals". Marianne was in Thornton Wilder's *Our Town*, and possibly in one of the group's open-air productions at Reading Abbey. At fifteen she also began singing folk songs in local clubs and coffee bars, such as Shades and Café-au-Lait. At home, where Eva refused to entertain the idea of having a record player—or telephone—in the house, she listened to jazz on the radio, and sometimes tuned into the French stations. For a time she emulated Existentialist icon Juliette Gréco with her beatnik hairstyle and clothes—the two later met and became friends. On weekends she travelled to London and visited the clubs there, almost always alone and speaking to no one: at the Marquee and Ronnie Scott's she saw Zoot Money and Nina Simone, and dreamed of one day becoming a famous singer herself. She compared this period in her life with what her mother had experienced during and immediately after the war: "It was as if I too had crawled out from under the rubble and, having survived the worst, I now wanted to have fun." Little did she know that, with the exception of Gréco and Callas, she would become a bigger name than any of the artistes she ever saw in London.

By the summer of 1962, Marianne's social calendar had been extended to attending university functions, and at a Cambridge ball she met the man she described as "my catalyst, my Virgil"—20-year-old Leighton Park student John Dunbar. It was love at first sight with someone from a background as suitably off-beat as her own—his father was the film-maker Robert, best known for the *Meet The Lyons* series with husband and wife team Ben Lyons and Bebe Daniels. His mother, Tatiana, was a

11

Russian émigré. Born in Mexico, Dunbar spent his first four years in Moscow. Looks-wise, he and Marianne were worlds apart: the fragile-looking, beautiful, fashion-conscious noblewoman's daughter —the geeky student with his unruly mop of dark hair, toothy grin, sloppy dress habits and horn-rimmed spectacles. Like Marianne, Dunbar was heavily into jazz. "He was my Pygmalion," she recalled, "And I was more than ready for him. I soaked it all up like a sponge." An intellectual with invaluable connection among London's social set, he introduced Marianne to Peter Asher—one half of singing duo Peter and Gordon, who had recently scored a big hit with "A World Without Love".

Through Asher, Marianne met Paul McCartney—lodging at the time with Asher's parents and engaged to his actress sister, Jane. More importantly Asher introduced her to the man who inspired and influenced her more than any other—Mick Jagger.

This prelude to Marianne's and Jagger's later monumental meeting—which she has always played down—took place in March 1964 when she and John Dunbar, guests of Peter Asher, attended a party in Paddington organised to launch the pop career of "hip chick" personality Adrienne Poster (later Posta). Poster, a teenage singer of limited ability whose latest, over-hyped single, "Only Fifteen" had bombed spectacularly (as would its successors), was currently being represented by Andrew Loog Oldham, the 20-year-old, flamboyant guru who managed The Rolling Stones—promoting their "bad boy" image to set them in competition with The Beatles. Oldham's tendency to wear make-up—and his fondness for turning up at public events looking like an androgynous gangster, addressing women and men alike as "darling"—is believed to have been but a ploy to seduce women, the idea being that their menfolk would slacken their guard, assuming him to be gay, whence he would make his move. With Oldham at the Posta launch party was his business partner, Tony Calder, the man who had promoted The Beatles' "Love Me Do".

Marianne claimed she was initially unimpressed by The Rolling Stones, recently returned from the Montreux Pop Festival—denouncing them as "not much more than yobby schoolboys" and lacking the polish of a Lennon or McCartney. Mick Jagger, she said, she would not have noticed at all had he not engaged in a ferocious argument with his girlfriend, Chrissie Shrimpton, younger sister of model Jean. Later, of course, she would revise her opinion.

In fact, Marianne had set her sights on Andrew Loog Oldham, who she describes in her memoirs as a man of "Wagnerian intensity", and who later observed of their meeting and his decision to make her a star, "I saw an angel with big tits, and signed her." It was apparently as simple as that. Oldham asked John Dunbar if his girlfriend could act or sing, before dismissing this as irrelevant. Marianne was possessed of a trait none of the other Brit Girls had, with the exception of Kathy Kirby and Sandie Shaw: exquisite looks—in her case an angular face framed by a cascade of shimmering blonde hair, a flawless complexion, a stunning figure and (Dusty aside) an impeccable cut-glass accent. Clearly, Oldham saw himself as a rival of Brian Epstein. And whereas Epstein had the Beatles and Cilla Black, who had recently celebrated her first Number

One, Oldham had The Stones, and now Marianne. She also proved easy to work with and mold to his requirements. It had all happened so quickly that so far as a pop career was concerned, she had no preconceived ideas of what would be expected of her. Also, to Oldham's boorish way of thinking, with so perfect a package, talent was secondary— though within hours he was discussing her debut single with Calder and the arranger, Mike Leander.

Former law student Leander (Mike Farr, 1941-96), had studied orchestration at Trinity College, and worked with Cliff Richard, Billy Fury, Shirley Bassey and Gene Pitney. Years later, Marianne denounced him as "insanely manipulative", and added of his genre, "A producer is a creature to fear—somebody who takes your gift and exploits it, or distorts it."

One week later, following a series of telegrams— Eva still refused to have a phone in the house— Marianne was summoned to Decca's Olympic Studios. The contract she was offered (signed by Eva because she was legally still a minor) would see her following in the footsteps of Joan Regan, Vera Lynn and Tommy Steele, to name but three. Present at the session were Oldham, Mick Jagger and Keith Richards—and Lionel Bart, who offered her his latest composition, "I Don't Know How To Tell You". She hated it, but went ahead with the session, recording several takes before giving up on it. Oldham then asked her to try another new song, written by Mick Jagger and Keith Richards: "As Time Go By" was their first original composition— until this point in their career, The Stones had covered mostly blues standards.

Almost certainly, the whole exercise of dragging Lionel Bart along to the session was a put-up job. Aware that Marianne would reject Bart's effort, Oldham had every intention of getting her to record the Jagger-Richards song, which he appears to have forced out of them—shutting the pair in his kitchen, giving them a two-hour deadline and the instruction, "I want a song with brick walls around it, high windows, and no sex." In the studio, he played Marianne a tape of Jagger on vocals, accompanied by an acoustic guitar. Someone—maybe her—pointed out that there was already a famous song with this title, performed by Dooley Wilson to Ingrid Bergman in *Casablanca*. The title was changed to "As *Tears* Go By", this single word-change Oldham's only contribution to the composition, whose name was added to the credits, as happened with the B-side, "Greensleeves", which effectively saw him sharing song-writing "honours" with Henry VIII!

Once she had rehearsed the song, Marianne laid down the vocals in just two takes. The Rolling Stones later recorded a pleasantly tender cover-version, and included it on the flipside of "19th Nervous Breakdown". Marianne's wistful delivery has unmistakable shades of Marie Laforet and Francoise Hardy, along with some of the breath control picked up from listening to Juliette Gréco. Like Laforet and Hardy (but never Gréco), and the later Nick Drake, Oldham achieved the best from her limited vocal powers by positioning her next to the microphone (and sometimes two), and this also gave her performances a breathy, more intimate edge. To say that it was written by two 20-year-olds for a 17-year-old, "As Tears Go By" is an unusually mature piece. Marianne sings it beautifully, of this there is no doubt, but many fans believed her later recording—when she had experienced more of life and was better suited to reflecting on her troubled past, at least part-orchestrated by one of the song's composers—to have been the better version. Released in June 1964, it was a slow mover—entering the charts in mid-August but eventually peaking at Number 9. Effectively, it gave Marianne the edge over her Brit Girl colleagues—a successful debut single after less than four months in the business, *and* a Number 22 hit in America.

"As Tears Go By" was launched on a Tyne-Tees Television music magazine. In her memoirs, Marianne recalls travelling up to Newcastle with Andrew Loog Oldham and Lionel Bart in the latter's sports car, and returning to London on the train, sharing a carriage with the actor-musician Jeremy Clyde—one half of Chad & Jeremy, whose only UK hit, "Yesterday's Gone", had just been released—and, that same night, Clyde's bed. She was still with John Dunbar, but also confesses to having had her first Sapphic experience, with a beautiful 16-year-old girl named Saida. "She gave me a Tuinal and seduced me in the flat I had moved into in Lennox Gardens," she recalled, having set a precedent for never accepting second-best and for wrenching as much out of life as possible.

When "As Tears Go By" hit the charts, Marianne left St Joseph's—the timing was perfect, close to the end of the summer term—and almost overnight she was temporarily gone from Eva Faithfull's life. In retrospect, this was a mistake….in the coming years

16

lovers and a few drug-addicted friends aside, she would have no one to lean on. She had led a fairly sheltered existence and was ill-prepared for entering the cut-throat world of the music business. John Dunbar was also absent: the pair had an argument, the first of many in their up-and-down relationship, and Dunbar had gone off to Greece for the summer. The first he would hear of Marianne's success would be upon his return to England, when he heard her on the radio.

Marianne was different from the other Brit Girls in that everyone assumed her to be as demure, shy and fragile as she looked, thus Andrew Oldham was initially reluctant to launch her on the tour circuit, wondering how she would cope with the frequently gruelling routine of being on the road, with little time for a social life. Her first tour, towards the end of 1964, was as part of a package which included The Hollies, Freddie & The Dreamers, The Four Pennies, and Gerry & The Pacemakers—a fun-loving bunch of young men who also must have been more than a little apprehensive of having an ex-convent schoolgirl in their midst, and of having to be mindful of their language and behaviour. "It was like being packed off in a submarine with the Manchester United football team," she recalled. Adding to the confusion was Oldham's press-release which concluded, "She likes Marlon Brando, Woodbine cigarettes, poetry, and going to the ballet. She loves to wear long evening dresses and is a shy, wistful girl with a waif-like beauty all of her own."

Chaperoned by an older friend, Marianne was put on an £80 a week retainer by her record company, in advance of royalties. Her "rocks" throughout the

17

tour were The Hollies' Graham Nash and Allan Clarke, of whom she confessed, "I'd have lunch with Graham, and spend the night with Allan."

Certainly it did not take Marianne long to fit in with the crowd. Some audiences, too, were quite hostile. Many of them had turned up at the theatre or cinema to listen to the latest beat groups, not some "posh girl novelty act" performing folk songs, and they made sure that she knew this, shouting and heckling when she was on stage. Her stage fright was so bad at times that she stood rooted to the spot, eyes closed, her arms hanging limply by her sides and completely unaware of her surroundings until she had finished her set. She persevered, and in the end with her innate charisma won them over.

Despite the success of "As Tears Go By", Marianne was convinced that she would go down in pop history as a one-hit-wonder. "I don't honestly like it all that much," she told a *Record Mirror* journalist of her debut single. Mike Leander, who appears to have had some sway over her, was working overseas and as Andrew Loog Oldham appears to have been in a world of his own much of the time, Marianne was given full control over the choice of material for her next single. Therefore in September 1964, Decca went along with her request to record Bob Dylan's civil rights-protest song, "Blowin' In The Wind", from his 1963 album, *The Freewheelin' Bob Dylan*. This had recently been a big hit for Peter, Paul & Mary, though by the time Marianne got around to covering it, it was more associated with Marlene Dietrich—she had recorded it in English, French and German, and would take it around the world on concert tours for many years to come. Marianne's reading owes much to the Dietrich recording, arranged by her then orchestra leader, Burt Bacharach. It is vibrant, exciting, and almost as brilliantly orchestrated—sadly, not what was expected of her immediately after charting with a Rolling Stones composition. For the B-side, Marianne chose "House Of The Rising Sun", a folk-song which had given The Animals a British Number One—Johnny Hallyday had topped the French charts with it, as "Le pénitentier".

Marianne's reading of the song owed more to the sultry English interpretation by Marie Laforet, her nearest French equivalent at the time. Born in 1939, Laforet was instrumental in popularizing Bob Dylan in Europe—and was regarded as the perfect anodine for the French yé-yé wave which superceded the age of The Twist. In 1966 she had a hit with "Marie-douceur, Marie-colere", her adaptation of The Stones' "Paint It Black", and further hits with Marianne's "Sha La La Song" and "Mary Ann".

Compared to Laforet's, Marianne's first recording of "House Of The Rising Sun" was lackluster—in her memoirs she herself dismisses *both* songs as "dreary", which is certainly not true. The record received more than its share of airplay—Marianne sang both songs on *Ready, Steady, Go!*—but it flopped just the same. And it was during the *RSG* post-show party that Mick Jagger famously slopped wine down the front of her dress, paving the way for one of the most talked about and controversial romances in British pop history.

19

Marianne, around the time she
recorded "As Tears Go By".

2: Tomorrow's Calling

Marianne was not just bored with her pop career— she was becoming increasingly disillusioned with what she called Andrew Loog Oldham's "fog-and-amphetamine factor". He was too hip for her, she said, and too fast: most of the time she had no idea what he was talking about. "He's sincere," she told one music journalist, "Well—he says so, so let's pretend he is." When "Blowin' In The Wind" failed to chart, she left Oldham, who in any case had his hands full managing the Rolling Stones, Herman's Hermits, and Chris Farlowe, and for a while she was managed by Oldham's business partner, Tony Calder, who she described as "a bit sleazy, but in the nicest possible way."

Truthfully, Marianne was not that enamoured of the music business in general, and had made it clear from the outset that she would never be pushed around. She had a very clear indication of what she wanted out of life, but as yet little idea of how to go about getting it. Soon after Calder took over, she was approached by the producer Anthony Page, who wanted her to audition for a part in John Osborne's new play, *Inadmissible Evidence*, starring Nicole Williamson and scheduled to open at the Royal Court Theatre in November. This, she said, she saw as a way out of her "pop nightmare". Calder—and Decca—persuaded her not to: he and the company stood to make a huge loss if all she was earning was £20 a week on the stage, opposed to what she could rake in on the tour circuit. Later, however, the opportunity would re-occur for her to work with Williamson.

It was Tony Calder who persuaded Marianne to record Jackie DeShannon's superb "Come And Stay With Me"—a bouncy, optimistic piece composed not, it would appear, in a kitchen this time but in a bedroom after a particularly noisy romp between DeShannon and her current amour, Jimmy Page, later of Yardbirds and Led Zeppelin fame. Page had worked as a session musician on "As Tears Go By". According to Marianne, she and Calder were sitting in the next room when Calder called out, "As soon as you two are finished fucking each other's brains out, why don't you write Marianne a song?" What they came up with was a chanson-within-pop plea: the girl will give up everything for the man she loves, and even allow him to have his freedom if this is what he wishes, just so long as he promises to move in with her. The record peaked at Number 4 in the UK charts, giving her what would be her biggest commercial hit. The flatly-delivered B-side, "What Have I Done Wrong?", which would have befitted a retake, was written especially for Marianne by Mike Leander, using his pseudonym (actually his real name) Mike Farr.

In the spring of 1965, Marianne—accompanied by her guitarist, Jon Mark—went on tour with the Kinks (who she described as "creepy and silent"), Gerry & The Pacemakers, and The Manish Boys: their frontman was David Jones, who became David Bowie. Mark (John Michael Burchell) was an accomplished musician who later joined John Mayall's Bluesbreakers, and in 1970 formed the duo Mark-Almond with Johnny Almond. Headlining the package was Gene Pitney, the Connecticut-born crooner with the squeaky voice and an unmistakable croak in the throat, with whom she embarked on a brief affair.

Pitney had topped the charts with "Twenty Four Hours From Tulsa", and had been present at the Rolling Stones' early recording sessions—some believe him to have played piano on their debut album. Jagger and Richards had written "That Girl Belongs To Yesterday" for him, and after his affair with Marianne—which saw her getting pregnant and having an abortion—José Duarte wrote him "Marianne", which contains the not so flattering lines, "It's so easy to love her, it's so easy to want her....the beginning of the end when you meet Marianne." Despite their romance, she does not beat about the bush when expressing her opinion of him. "He was absolutely the most pompous, self-satisfied person you could ever imagine," she observes in *Faithfull*. "He took himself so deadly serious that it was actually funny....He was a good fuck and I was a very young girl getting as much experience as I could, as fast as possible." In her later *Memories, Dreams & Reflections*, she would be slightly more reverent when writing of Pitney's sudden death, "The odds of Gene dying in Cardiff—poor sod—are astronomical. I give him all honour and credit for the work he did, but what a place to shuffle off your mortal coil."

Marianne disliked touring, telling the *New Musical Express*, "I hate leaving home, I hate the travelling, I hate the packing. I hate it!" This was one of her less-complicated outbursts. To other journalists, her responses to otherwise innocuous questions, such as what was her favourite colour, or food, were ambiguous, and convoluted. In the four-letter-word world of the tour circuit, they were presented with a girl who could articulate, quote the classics, and outfox them. Polite reporters would be offered little gifts, such as second-hand signed copies of her favourite books. Interviewed in a London park by *Record Mirror's* Richard Green who asked her what her aspirations were for the future, she bamboozled him with the prognosis, "When I'm so rich that I don't have to make more than one good record a year, I'll have a house in Venice and a place in the Greek Islands. I'll be a female Beatle and only come over to England to do television and concerts." Much more controversially Marianne perceived herself as the female captain of an imaginary pirate radio ship—the *Marijuana*—in which she would smuggle liquor and tobacco into the country. She made it very clear to Keith Altham of the *New Musical Express* that she was not the sort of girl who hung around draughty studios waiting to be interviewed—if he really wanted to chat to her, then it would be over lunch at a fancy London club. "Marianne never does what a pop star does," Altham observed in April 1965, "She has a pert, child-like face which darts out at you from a cascade of fine, fair hair....When she is pleased, her whole face dimples into an uninhibited smile, and she plays at being sex-kitten and society hostess in turn." The waiter looked down his nose when she dismissed everything on the costly menu and asked for sausage and mash. After the interview—most of the time she complained about Andrew Loog Oldham, blaming him for saddling her with "Blowing In The Wind", when *she* had chosen this, Marianne expressed her gratitude, by asking Altham to wait outside the book shop across the road while she dashed inside and bought him a little gift: A P Herbert's *Big Ben, A Light Opera In Two Acts*!

In the wake of the failed single, Marianne dropped Tony Calder and was signed by Gerry Bron, brother of actress Eleanor and manager of the Bonzo Dog Doo-Dah Band, Manfred Mann, and Gene Pitney—he had recently produced his "Something's Gotten Hold Of My Heart". Bron sent her on tour with Roy Orbison, who after breaking his foot in a motorcycle accident performed much of the time wearing a cast. Marianne described him as looking "like a prodigal mole in Tony Lama cowboy boots"—and promptly turned down his amorous advances. To complicate matters, during this tour—in Wigan, on its famous pier—John Dunbar, horrified by tabloid reports of the Faithfull-Pitney affair and in what appears to have been an attempt to "make her decent again", asked Marianne to marry him. She readily accepted, actually believing that things would work out better between them once his ring was on her finger. "The convent girl reappeared," she recalled, "I started to think I was a bad woman, a whore and a slut, I'd better get married and then I'd be good again." The tabloids which had criticised Marianne subsequently turned on her fiancé—Dunbar, absent during her rapid ascendency to pop fame, was now perceived as the gold-digger who had suddenly appeared from nowhere. Eva Faithfull certainly saw him in this light, and is known to have disliked him, possibly because, unaware of the whole story, she believed *he* may have been leading her daughter astray. The news of the wedding coincided with Marianne's announcement that she was pregnant.

25

Meanwhile on 26 April 1965, in Marianne's own words, "God himself checked into the Savoy Hotel." She was one of the many artistes and musicians who made the pilgrimage (in her case almost every day for two weeks) to the establishment, where in the middle of a three-week tour, seminal songwriter Bob Dylan was holding court. The sojourn had been arranged by his manager, Albert Grossman, and the film director D A Pennebaker—the idea being that the comings and goings would be recorded for posterity by the cameras which rolled day and night. The footage was edited into the tacky, copiously vulgar documentary *Don't Look Back* which charted Dylan's self-importance but undisputed influence on fellow musicians and camp-followers. Present much of the time was his then-lover, Joan Baez, and wafting into the strands of his life throughout the course of the film in an atmosphere heavy with pot smoke were "friends" such as folk singers Donovan and Dana Gillespie, the Animals' Alan Price, beat poet Allen Ginsberg, and a blink-and-miss-her Marianne—all hoping to gain some clout, in the near future, by being seen to be worshipping at his oracle. Most of the time, Dylan stumbled about the hotel suite looking neo-mystical: alternatively he would sit hunched over his typewriter into which, emulating Jack Kerouac, he had inserted an Izal toilet-roll so that he could tap out whatever random lyrics came into his head. Neither does Marianne appear to have been averse to wanting to sleep with him, should he have wished for this to happen, later observing how the traditional tribute offered by female fans to such legends was usually themselves.

"John was still at Cambridge doing his finals and wouldn't be back for a while," she recalled, "And what he didn't know might not hurt him." This did not happen. When Marianne told Dylan she was to be married, and that her husband-to-be was an English poet—he asked, "Can he write poems about monkey wrenches and atomic alarm clocks and fat black mamas?" Then, having opined that only undertakers and college professors wore glasses, he expressed his disapproval of Dunbar by growling, "What d'ya want to marry a damn student for?"

Perhaps by marrying Marianne, Dunbar believed that, as any prospective bridegroom would, from now on he would have her all to himself. Also, the reason for the wedding, which it was announced would take place as soon as there was a gap in Marianne's hectic schedule, may have had as much to do with her record company not wanting to have an 18-year-old unmarried mother on their hands, and risk losing their investment at a time when such things were frowned upon. The wedding took place on 6 May 1965 at the Cambridge Registry Office. Marianne carried a bouquet of wild flowers and May-blossom which she and Dunbar had picked from a nearby field, but as the ceremony was not conducted by a Catholic priest Eva Faithfull refused to recognise the marriage and a second ceremony, attended by her and Marianne's father, took place six weeks later at St Mary's Church, Knightsbridge. Peter Asher was best man, and guests of honour were Asher's singing partner, Gordon Waller, "My Boy Lollipop" girl Millie Small, and Marianne's close friend Barry Fantoni, the musician and editor of *Private Eye* who always carried a torch for her.

After the first ceremony, Dunbar arguably made a rod for his own back by telling a reporter from the *Cambridge Evening News*, "Marianne will keep on singing,"—hinting, wrongly, that he was the one who wore the trousers in their relationship and that she would have to seek *his* approval to continue with her career. Her tongue-in-cheek statement, believed at the time, was that she and her new husband would be moving to Cornwall, where they hoped to raise six children. Later, she expressed no little bitterness when she observed, "He'd got the goose that laid the golden egg, and knew it. Never have to work again." There was a brief honeymoon in Paris where the couple spent time with beat poets Allen Ginsberg and Gregory Corso. Marianne formed a deep bond of friendship with both—Corso often referred to her as his "great unconsummated love affair".

Home for the Dunbars was Marianne's flat in Chelsea, which over the next few months became a drugs-party haven and meeting place for musicians and intellectuals from all walks of life: Ginsberg and Corso, controversial Polish film director Roman Polanski—and Eva Faithfull. Marianne was preparing for her biggest challenge so far. Decca were pressing her to record and release a debut pop album, whereas she wanted to record an album of folk songs. She offered no compromise, not even when the record company suggested an album containing both genres: she had never failed to remind those about her how much she disliked the music business, and if she was going to stay a part of it, then it would be under her own terms. Decca would have their album, but she would have hers.

John Dunbar, meanwhile, tried to earn his crust as best he could, while studying for his final exams—writing a fortnightly column for *The Scotsman*, and with a friend called Barry Miles (it is believed with financial input from Marianne, and Peter Asher) opening the Indica Gallery in the basement of a bookshop they opened in Mason's Yard, Mayfair. This staged exhibits by "cutting edge" artists—here, in November 1966, Dunbar introduced John Lennon to Yoko Ono during a tacky exhibition of her paintings and other works—one such was an apple, perched on a pedestal with a £200 price tag attached to it—another a piece of wood with nails in it, and the printed request for the viewer to hammer in more of the same. The following year, perhaps not surprisingly, the enterprise folded and Dunbar himself became an artist.

The albums were both released on 15 April 1965. *Marianne Faithfull* opens with "Come And Stay With Me", which leads nicely into Bacharach and David's excellent "If I Never Get To Love You". Cilla Black, Dusty Springfield and Dionne Warwick –first in line with their songs—somehow missed out on this one, originally recorded by the little-known Lou Johnson, though there was a more successful if not aggressive version by Timi Yuro. From the double-bass intro, as performed by Marianne this is a bright, breezy and optimistic piece, delivered with assumed innocence and effective backing vocals. Next up is Marianne's own "Time Takes Time", a poem set to music by her friend and would-be suitor, Barry Fantoni. "The wind laughs, and the world cries....but I don't care anymore," she wistfully opines.

"He'll Come Back To Me" was Mike Leander's adaptation of a French song, "A bientot nous deux", written by Robert Gall—one of Edith Piaf's last composers—for his 16-year-old daughter, France, who won the Eurovision Song Contest the following year with his and Serge Gainsbourg's "Poupée de cire, poupée de son". The arrangement is almost identical to the original, the performance (Marianne also recorded it in French) far superior. Sadly, the same cannot be said for her interpretation of Tony Hatch's "Down Town", written after his first visit to New York—intentionally for the Drifters, until he had changed his mind and given it to Petula Clark, who had taken it to the top of the charts on both sides of the Atlantic. Whereas Petula's coarse, strident tones are more in keeping with the hustle-bustle theme of the city that never sleeps, Marianne's reading of the song is merely passable. "Plaisir d'amour", on the other hand, is exquisite. Written in 1780 by Jean de Florian and beautifully set to music by Jean-Paul Martini, there have been notable renditions by Nana Mouskouri, Tino Rossi and Fritz Wunderlitz. Marianne's, accompanied by Jon Mark on the acoustic guitar, takes in the complicated key changes whilst adhering to the original sheet music. Ken Lewis and John Carter's "Can't You Hear My Heartbeat?" had provided Goldie and the Gingerbreads with their only British hit: a cover version by Herman's Hermits, not released in the UK, had reached Number 2 on the *Billboard* chart. Again, Marianne gives the better interpretation—every now and then she tosses a sexy little "Ooh!" into the mix, bringing Side One to a very pleasant close.

Side Two of *Marianne Faithfull* opens with "As Tears Go By". Then comes Jon Birchell's beautiful tone poem, "Paris Bells", popular at the time with television audiences. Accompanied by Jon Mark and backed by a stunning humming chorus, the narrator wanders around Paris reflecting on the wedding that was not to be but which, within her mind, like the sound of the church bells lingers still. "They Will Never Leave You" is Tony Calder's English adaptation of "Emporte avec toi", a hit in France for singer-songwriter Jean-Jacques Debout which has shades of the popular song, "Étoile des neiges". "What Have They Done To The Rain?" a hit for the Searchers, is much more suited to Marianne's then Dylanesque approach to her work than it was to theirs. Penned in 1962 by American blues singer Malvina Reynolds—who wrote "Little Boxes" for Pete Seeger—this was a protest against nuclear testing, though Marianne turns it into a gently effective, otherwise innocuous folk song. In the wake of the staggering success of "Come And Stay With Me", Jackie DeShannon had collaborated with Jimmy Page to furnish Marianne with "In My Time Of Sorrow", a bleak piece which she handles well despite her youth. The subject, a heavy one for a life-loving 18-year-old, is the contemplation of suicide. After "What Have I Done Wrong?" Marianne rounds off the proceedings with Lennon and McCartney's "I'm A Loser", from the *Beatles For Sale* album. According to John Lennon, the song was not about *losing* a lover, but being a loser in life. "Is it for him, or myself that I cry?" she asks herself. Two other tracks were recorded for the album: the traditional folk song "All My Trials" and

31

Phil Ochs' magnificent pastiche, "There But For Fortune". Marianne sang both songs beautifully on the television, but the recordings were tragically assigned to the Decca vaults, from which they have never emerged.

Come My Way is not just an album, but a work of art: even the cover was eclectic, a monochrome shot by her friend Chris O'Dell (who her mother had taken in as a child) which depicts Marianne reclining in a pub, wearing a dark dress and white knee-socks. Purists tried to argue that she was neither pop star nor folk singer—too sultry for one genre, not vocally suited for the other. Obviously they had never heard of Continental counterparts Francoise Hardy and Marie Laforet, and now she was about to prove them wrong! Not many teenage entertainers were capable of doing what she had done in this album, let alone of doing it inordinately well. The superb title-track is by Jon Mark, who accompanies her throughout. In it Marianne wishes for everyone to find happiness and joy, though this has evaded her, therefore she implores these lovers, "Sometimes spare a thought of me and say, 'Love, come her way!'" Next comes "Jaberwock", a spoken interpretation of Lewis Carroll's nonsense poem "Jabberwocky", from *Through The Looking Glass*. Next is "Portland Town", the moving tale of the Oregon mother whose three sons have all died fighting for their country. This had been written in 1957 by the American poet Derroll Adams, who when Marianne recorded his song was mentoring Donovan Leitch. After the folk version of "House Of The Rising Sun" comes the beautifully sung "Spanish Is A Loving Tongue", by the cowboy poet,

Charles Badger Clark Jr. Marianne's diction as always with this type of song (though not always in her early pop numbers) is pronounced and clear. A man's song, this tells of the white man who falls in love with the Mexican girl, a love which is doomed from the start because of racial prejudice. After the equally splendid "Fare Thee Well", an exercise in unadulterated folk perfection placing Marianne on the same level as Joan Baez, with her voice rising flute-like a whole octave, the first side of the album closes with a hesitant "Lonesome Traveler", the old Kingston Trio number, composed by John Hays and which had seen a revival since the publication of Jack Kerouac's novel of the same title, based on his road diaries.

Side Two opens with a sterling interpretation of the English classic, "Down In The Salley Garden": based on the 1889 poem by William Butler Yeats, the *salley* in the title refers to the willow tree. "Mary Ann", a sad piece, tells of the sailor's pain of saying goodbye to his girl, which he equates with that of the fish on the hook, and the lobster boiling in the pot. "Full Fathom Five", the album's second spoken selection, is the song which Ariel pronounces in *The Tempest*—and also the title of a novel by Ahmad Kamal, a poem by Sylvia Plath, a painting by Jackson Pollock, and a classical work by Vaughan Williams! With it, Marianne displays her dramatic acting skills which would soon be put to good use. "Four Strong Winds", perhaps the best song on this album, was written by Canadian folk singer Ian Tyson, and introduced by the harmony group, The Brothers Four. Whereas they drawl the lyrics, Marianne brings them to life. Of the same quality is her interpretation of "Black Girl", also known as "The Pines", an American folk song dating back to 1870. There have been many variants, depending on the ethnic sensibilities of the artist performing it, though the theme is the same—prejudiced questions levelled at a black woman accused of wrongdoing, and her truthful response which is not disbelieved by all. Bob Dylan had performed it at Carnegie Hall. Next up, Marianne laments the loss of her lover in "Once I Had A Sweetheart", before ending this masterly collection with "Bells Of Freedom". "Way across the deep blue ocean, way above the mountains so high," she optimistically proclaims, "Come friends and people from every corner, people from everywhere!"

Both albums entered the UK charts during the first week of June 1965. *Marianne Faithfull* peaked at a healthy Number 15, but *Come My Way* did even better, reaching Number 12—proving to Marianne that she really did have what it took to be a high-ranking folk singer. Meanwhile, on 24, 25 and 26 May, she participated in a one-off showcase: The Brighton Song Festival. This comprised two heats, and a grand final. Her fellow competitors were Dave Berry, Cliff Bennett & The Rebel Rousers, Maureen Evans, The Ivy League, Kenny Lynch, The Moody Blues, Helen Shapiro, Elkie Brooks, Wayne Fontana, Billy J Kramer, Lulu, Manfred Mann, July Rogers, and Mark Wynter. Stiff competition indeed, and Marianne's entry was a cracker—Jon Mark's "Go Away From My World", orchestrated by Mike Leander and arguably her best song that year. Indeed, it could almost be regarded as her creed—the relationship which has not worked out, therefore the lover—or maybe husband John Dunbar—is asked to go away so that she can dream of how *she* wanted it to be. "Can't you see it never worked from the start?" she asks in a voice so pure, yet heavy with longing. For ridiculous reasons known only to them, Decca opted not to release it as a single, but on an EP with "The Sha La La Song", "The Most Of What Is Least", and Gilbert Bécaud's "Et maintenant" which Marianne performs in near-flawless French and to Bécaud's own heavy drums, horn and penny-whistle arrangement. During the Spring of 1965 she included this in her five-song set at the Paris Olympia. "Go Away From My World" was one of the selections she performed live on the BBC Light Programme's *Saturday Club*, presented by Brian Matthew. Marianne won the first heat of the contest outright—way ahead of everyone else—but in the final was pipped to the post by Kenny Lynch's instantly forgettable "I'll Stay By You", whilst Marianne's song is today regarded as a timeless classic.

The *Saturday Club* performances, five of these between 13 May 1965 and 31 May 1966, comprising fifteen songs—some accompanied by the Mike Leander Orchestra, others just by Jon Mark—were believed lost until 2007 when the tapes were discovered in a Decca vault, cleaned up, and released the following year on a CD, *Marianne Faithfull: Live At The BBC*. Each musical interlude was preceded by a brief, "butter-wouldn't melt" interview—not that Marianne gave much away about her private life, for in these days presenters and to a certain extent music journalists were far more interested in the music, than in what may have

35

been happening behind closed doors. Only once does Brian Matthew fly too close to the sun by asking her about her "secret" marriage—to be politely told that this was of no one's concern but her own. Obviously, only those closest to her were aware on 31 May of her biggest secret—that she was pregnant. During one of these interviews she also gave an insight into her ambitions: she wanted to make a modern jazz album, and to act and make films. "Is this something that you just want to do, or that you may well do?" Matthew asked, bringing the hushed response, "It's something that I'm putting myself into the position of occurring!"

Marianne's next single, "This Little Bird", came courtesy of Tennessee Williams. In his 1957 play, *Orpheus Descending* (itself a near complete rewrite of his earlier *Battle of Angels*), the central character Val Xavier delivers a monologue referring to the bird which sleeps on the wind, and only touches the ground when it dies. Williams' script was adapted and set to music by John D Loudermilk, whose past credits included "Sittin' On The Balcony" for Eddie Cochran. There was competition by way of a rival version by the Nashville Teens, despite their name a British pop group who had recently had a hit with "Tobacco Road", also by Loudermilk. What made this rival version unusual, if not spiteful, was that it was also released by Decca and produced by Andrew Loog Oldham—almost certainly his way of getting back at Marianne for dropping him. "Some negative people say that I have malicious intent," Oldham told *Record Mirror*, "All I say is that *evil*, as well as beauty, is obviously in the eye of the beholder." If so, it was a wasted exercise—while the

Nashville Teens' record barely edged into the Top 40, Marianne's reached Number 6. At just two-minutes it remains one of her shortest songs, but one of her most beautiful.

Marianne intended working as far into her pregnancy as possible. She continued touring, and in June appeared at the Uxbridge Blues and Folk Festival. Then, during a concert in Morecambe she collapsed from exhaustion, and the remaining dates in her current schedule were cancelled on doctor's orders—including a tour of America (where she was to share equal billing with the Byrds), where *Marianne Faithfull* had reached Number 12 in the album charts. For each of these shows, Gerry Bron had demanded a non-negotiable $1,000 fee, and upon learning that the tour would have to be shelved the promoter upped this to $1,500 in the hope of tempting Marianne across the Atlantic, to no avail.

In July 1965 ahead of the proposed tour, Marianne had recorded Brian Thomas Henderson's "Summer Nights", one of her catchiest and for the time most topical songs. She first recorded it in French—as "Nuits d'été" it was a hit in Europe—and in Britain reached Number 10 in the charts. From its effective harpsichord intro to the fade-out ending, the song brings to mind Marie Laforet's aforementioned "Les vendanges de l'amour"—the fact that the dreary winter is over, and the lovers can now head off for their favourite summer haunts and pastimes, be this dancing in some little café, or just walking along the beach when day is done. On the flipside was Mike Leander's "The Sha La La Song", which Laforet liked so much that she recorded it in French (A demain my darling), and Italian (A domane amore).

Marianne rounded off an excellent year with Lennon and McCartney's "Yesterday", which according to *The Guinness Book of Records* has more cover-versions (over 3,000) of any song ever written: from Elvis Presley to Placido Domingo, from Liberace to Daffy Duck. Marianne's, with her own "Oh, Look Around You" on the flipside, certainly ranks among the top few, backed by Mike Leander's orchestra and 300 singers from the Royal College of Music. It was the first Beatles song to feature a solo (by McCartney), and allegedly came to him during a dream at Jane Asher's home. The group recorded it in June 1965—after the version by Matt Monroe, which reached Number 8 in the charts. Marianne's just made it into the Top 40, and sadly it would be one of her last commercial hits, though it by no means signaled the end of the road for her. Of her Brit Girl colleagues, Cilla and Dusty had topped the record sales charts in 1964, and Sandie Shaw would do so in 1965—with Marianne coming a close second, followed by Lulu, despite there having been no Number Ones. Artistically, she would outlive them all.

Singing "This Little Bird" on *Shindig*.

Marianne and John Dunbar.

3: Mick: The Butterfly On The Wheel

On 10 November 1965, at a Harley Street clinic, Marianne gave birth to a son—"the light of my life"—who she and John Dunbar baptised Nicholas. "I looked down at Nicholas, and decided that maybe there was a God after all," she recalled. "I wondered how something so pure could come into a cruel, imperfect world. Nicholas gazed back at me with the eyes of a very old soul indeed. He had the answer, but he wasn't telling." Nicholas was born prematurely, in the wake of an accident at Lennox Gardens when she had taken a tumble, but he was a healthy baby and doctors at the clinic reassured Marianne that there was no cause for concern. One of the first well-wishers was Andrew Loog Oldham, who called her from New York and asked her to get out of bed and glance out of her room window—parked outside was a gleaming new Mini, which many interpreted as Oldham's way of absolving his conscience after the "This Little Bird" saga.

The birth of their son more or less put paid to Marianne's marriage to John Dunbar. His idea of normality, she said, was to start off the day by adding liquid methadrine to his coffee—and end each one with a drug party at Lennox Gardens, where she was not allowed so much as a single spliff. She would get up on a morning, she added, and find herself stepping over the prostrate forms of crashed-out guests in the living room, then find the kitchen draining-board littered with blooded syringes. "Life was quietly becoming nightmarish," she concluded, "I was the wife and the mother and the golden goose, the one making the money to buy this stuff they were all doing." She had announced a six-month hiatus in her career, but her escalating popularity saw her returning to work almost at once, leaving Nicholas to be cared for by his nanny. Now almost entirely turned over to folk, she entered the studio and cut her most accomplished album of the genre, *North Country Maid*, which Decca released in April. Each song, brilliantly arranged by guitarists Jon Mark and Jim Sullivan, is impeccably delivered in a clear unwavering contralto not always evident in her pop songs. The album failed to chart, but by now Marianne had probably resigned herself to the fact that, like Helen Shapiro and Dusty, henceforth she would primarily be regarded as an album and concert artiste.

North Country Maid opens with Bert Jansch's "Green Are Your Eyes". Accompanied by just her guitarists, on either side of a sassy harmonica solo she gives an accomplished reading, the subject part-autobiographical in Marianne's case in that it involves the narrator keeping her wedding day a secret from her family. Next comes "Scarborough Fair", dating back to the 15th century and recently popularised by Simon & Garfunkel and Nana Mouskouri. The song tells of the man asking his friend to give his sweetheart a series of nigh-impossible tasks, upon the completion of which she will prove worthy of his love. The "parsley, sage, rosemary and thyme" is a 19th century addition to the original lyric—no one knows exactly what it means. "Cockleshells" is by Mick Taylor, who three years later replaced Brian Jones as the Rolling Stones' guitarist. She recorded it in French as "Coquillages" and it was released on an EP with "Si demain (The Sha La La Song), "Ne me quitte pas" (not the Brel song, but the theme from the film, *Les parapluies de Cherbourg*), and "Le coeur gros", an original song which Marianne never sang in English. After Tom Paxton's "The Last Thing On Mind" comes Ewan McColl's "The First Time Ever I Saw Your Face", without any doubt the finest folk song Marianne ever sang and possibly the definitive version of this beautiful work. When Marianne comes in on the wings of the mournful double-bass introduction, her voice crystal clear and soaring way above its usual limited range, the hairs on the back of one's neck stand on end. This first side closes with "Sally Free And Easy", the story of the flirt who took a man's love for granted once too often, and who now must pay the price. It was composed by West Country folk singer Cyril Tawney, and originally recorded by Carolyn Hester—again, it is much better performed here.

Side Two opens with "Sunny Goodge Street", written by Donovan and from his 1965 *Fairytale* album. This is a good song, but out of place here—telling of a drug-fuelled series of events which take place at the London underground station which doubtless only made sense, beyond the lengthy harmonica introduction, to the man who wrote it. After it comes another oddity, the first of Ophelia's "Mad Songs" from *Hamlet*—Marianne later played her on the stage. Extremely moving is her reading of "She Moved Thru The Fair", a traditional Irish song whose lyric here dates from 1922—in 1990, Marianne would reprise it for her *Blazing Away* album and tour. The title-track is stunning, yet for some reason is placed towards the end of the album:

the tale of the North Country maid who comes "up" (not down!) to London, laments doing so, yet may not return home until she has met another displaced Northerner who will marry her and carry her back to where she came from! Next comes Jon Mark's "Lullaby", written in honour of Nicholas—and Mark's own daughter, Francesca, born at around the same time. Rarely had Marianne given such an enchanting performance. And the album rounds off in spectacular fashion with Francis McPeake's "Wild Mountain Thyme", a "traditional Scots song" written by an Irishman! This time, it is the man who promises his "lassie" all kinds of wonderful things if she will travel North with him and pluck the wild mountain thyme—and if she turns down his offer, well, he will find someone else to accompany him! Like "She Moved Thru The Fair", this one sees Marianne unusually accompanied by the sitar.

There were also two very fine singles which, sadly, failed to chart. "Tomorrow's Calling" is an optimistic piece (the French version, "Si demain", even more so) was written for Marianne by Scots folk singer Eric Woolfson, later a co-founder of The Alan Parsons Project who also wrote for Frank Ifield and French singer Joe Dassin, and who worked at the time with the then little-known Andrew Lloyd Webber and Tim Rice. On the flipside was Marianne's own "That's Right Baby", described by Tim Tooher in the sleeve notes of the re-released (2007) *Come My Way* as sounding "like something from the soundtrack to some never made Tony Curtis spy romp." Gorgeous is the only way of describing "Counting", by Maryland troubadour Bob Lind. The arrangement is by Jack Nitzsche—he worked with the Rolling Stones at this time, which was probably how Marianne came to be offered this underrated gem, one of the most prosaic lyrics she ever sang. "Counting times you have stood at the foot of my ivory tower and waited and called out my name by the hour....And now between twilight and midnight I come to you, down in my gown of soft moonbeams and starlight..." Absolute heaven!

Marianne had cameo appearances in two eminent French films at this time. Jean-Luc Goddard was so enamoured of "As Tears Go By" that he asked her to sing this, *a capella*, in *Made In The USA*, which tells of a female private detective (Anna Karina) searching for her boyfriend's killers in Atlantic City. Karina suggested that Marianne should have a part in her next film, *Anna*, a television comedy-drama directed by Pierre Koralnik in which she starred with Jean-Claude Brialy and the *chansonnier*, Serge Gainsbourg. This centres around Brialy's obsession with a girl he has seen in a photograph. Marianne played "la jeune fille du dancing", and there was talk of her singing the theme-song, Gainsbourg's "Sous le ciel exactement", but this honour went to Karina. Instead she was given his "Hier oú demain", a delightful little piece which she performs looking very fragile, whilst being encircled by Brialy, who rudely blows smoke in her face. The film was a central component of *Montréal Expo 67*, where it proved so popular, largely on account of the Gainsbourg-Karina song, that it was screened twelve times a day! "Hier ou demain" was put out on a French EP to coincide with the film's release, along with three songs from the *North Country Maid*, and was a Top 30 hit in France.

It was now that Mick Jagger entered Marianne's life. During the early part of 1966, she spent a great deal of time with Brian Jones and Anita Pallenberg, the angelic looking Rolling Stones guitarist and his fiery Italian-German actress girlfriend possessed of no talent in particular, and a penchant for murdering the English language. The couple, who had met during the Stones' tour of Germany the previous year, shared a flat off London's Courtfield Road—described by Marianne as, "A veritable witches' coven of decadent illuminati, rock princelings and hip aristos....a hipness, decadence and exquisite tailoring such as England had not seen since the Restoration of Charles II." Keith Richards was almost a permanent fixture here, and these people all shared the same enthusiasm for drugs—and a disapproval of monogamy in these swinging, sexually liberated times. Marianne is said to have had her eye on Jones, primarily because she considered him the more intelligent (an IQ of 133) and cultured than the rest of the group. In 1974 (a story repeated by Mark Hodkinson) she claimed to have slept with him, but in her 1994 memoirs writes that his attempts to seduce her failed because "he was doing a lot of Mandrax, which rendered him even more wobbly than he already was."

Initially, Marianne is believed to have resisted Jagger's advances—she still found him crude, and seems to have been anxious to hang on to her marriage. However, having inherited her mother's rebellious nature, after her sedentary life with John Dunbar she was unable to resist the magnetic anodyne to boredom prescribed by this exciting, glamorous 22-year-old millionaire, already regarded as one of the greatest rock icons of all time.

The Jagger-Faithfull affair began after a Stones concert at Bristol's Colston Hall on 7 October 1966, where they were supported by Ike and Tina Turner. She was driven to the venue by one of her roadies, but after the show—which she described as "clinical Dionysian mass hysteria", she sent the roadie back to London, having decided to attend the all-night party at the city's Ship Hotel. Here, a huge quantity of drugs were consumed—nothing heavier than "grass, acid, and the occasional leaper," according to Marianne. Gradually, the guests paired up with whoever took their fancy and left, until she and Jagger were the only ones remaining. Following a dawn walk in a local park to help clear their drug-addled thoughts, they retired to Jagger's room, and so began one of the most controversial, talked about romances of the 20th century.

One week later, feeling guilty and needing to work out which man she belonged with, Marianne and Nicholas, accompanied by the child's nanny and a black model friend Marianne had recently met in a boutique and on the spur of the moment invited to join her party, flew to Paris. She later said how she had been unable to resist sleeping with the woman's boyfriend. In Paris, a letter awaited her from Dunbar, begging her to return home. Instead, she headed for Positano, on Italy's Amalfi Coast. From here, the party sailed across the Bay of Naples to Ischia—Jagger had found out about her plans, and when she arrived here a batch of letters awaited her from him. Two weeks later, having allowed Jagger to sweat things out and leaving everyone to make their way home, via the longer route, by car over the

Alps, Marianne flew back to London—but instead of returning to Lennox Gardens checked in at the Mayfair Hotel. From here she called Keith Richard, then promptly rushed to his flat and spent the night with him because, despite what had happened in Bristol, Richards was still the Rolling Stone she fancied the most! It was, she recalled, the best sex she had ever had in her life. Only then did she return to Jagger and, taking her time, she slowly allowed their relationship to develop. At this stage neither of them wanted to go public—on Jagger's part primarily because he had yet to break up with Chrissie Shrimpton.

The affair was brought into the open a few days before the Christmas of 1966, when Jagger and Shrimpton were scheduled to fly out to Jamaica for the festive season. It later emerged that he had called the airport and cancelled the tickets, and that somehow the press had got hold of this information and begun trailing him—on the day he should have been jetting off to the sun, Jagger was photographed entering Harrods with Marianne clinging to his arm. Not long afterwards, Shrimpton was admitted to a nursing home, following what the tabloids reported to have been a suicide attempt. Jagger's reaction was to have her personal effects removed from his home—then, while Shrimpton was recovering and John Dunbar licking his wounds, show business's hottest new couple set off on a cruise of the French Riviera. Their relationship, Marianne said, brought her freedom from a pop career she felt was hanging like a millstone around her neck. "Once I became Mick's girlfriend I no longer had to work, not for the money anyway," she said. "I could do *The Three*

47

Sisters for just £18 a week and not give a damn." Jagger was attentive and exciting, she added, while her husband was unworldly, selfish, and incapable of earning a living for himself. Jagger also appears to have been aware of Marianne's night of passion with Keith Richards—and to have fantasised about having sex with both of them. She remembered the occasion she had been in bed with Jagger, whilst Richards had been sleeping in the next room. As a prelude to sex, Jagger proclaimed his "homoerotic yearning" loud enough for his friend to hear every word: "If Keith were here right now, God, I'd like to lick him all over and then...then I'd suck his cock."

Not all of the couple's friends approved. Barry Fantoni denounced the Stones as, "All middle class yobs—except for Charlie and Bill, who were just yobs. Brian was brighter, but he suffered. He was much too sensitive." Of Jagger he told Marianne's biographer, Mark Hodkinson. "I think Mick is a deeply unpleasant person and I feel there is something quite repellent about his personality....he had great power and I think Marianne was seduced by that." Fantoni was so enamoured of Marianne that he may have been jealous of Jagger—who in any case could not be accused of leading Marianne astray and *making* her fall in love with him!

The couple's affair was brought to the attention of an international audience in January 1967, when Marianne participated in the San Remo Song Festival. This year's competition would go down in history less for the songs performed here than for the media interest in four of the singers' love lives: Marianne and Jagger—and Franco-Italian *chanteuse* Dalida's romance with the Italian singer-songwriter heartthrob, Luigi Tenco. Marianne, wearing a man's suit and paired with Ricky Maiocchi, performed "C'e chi spera", whilst Dalida and Tenco sang "Ciao amore ciao". Both songs were eliminated before the final, and according to media reports Tenco was so incensed by what he called the rigged voting that he retired to the room he was sharing with Dalida—the pair had just announced their marriage plans—and put a bullet into his skull, though some theorists still believe that his death, at just twenty-eight, was not suicide but murder, and the inquest into the tragedy persists to this day. Despite sterling competition from Gene Pitney, Sergio Endrigo and Connie Francis, the overall winners were Iva Zanicchi and Claudio Villa, who performed "Non pensare a me". The Tenco song became a posthumous Number One for him and a million-seller for Dalida—who twenty years later took her own life—whereas Marianne's entry, an absolutely brilliant song, has faded into obscurity. The world's press, which swooped on San Remo on 29 January, were interested only in the Tenco tragedy which was headline news across Europe for over a month. There were however a few British tabloid reporters in Italy, including Don Short of the *Daily Mirror*, who interviewed Jagger and Marianne and photographed them at the festival before they left the town to hire a yacht and cruise the French Riviera.

Marianne and Jagger returned to London, where she and Nicholas moved into Jagger's flat at Harley House, the opulent Victorian mansion block on Marylebone Road. Nowadays, luxury apartments there fetch up to £2 million, but in the mid-Sixties Jagger rented the place for just £50 a week. In case things did not work out between them, Marianne had decided to hang on to her own flat in Lennox Gardens. With no commitments over coming weeks she spent much of her time with the Rolling Stones, who were promoting their just-released fifth album, *Between The Buttons*, their last with Andrew Loog Oldham at the helm. The tracks on this included "Let's Spend The Night Together", Jagger's account of his escapade with Marianne at the Bristol hotel. It was notoriously banned by many radio stations and more famously resulted in a bust-up between Jagger and Ed Sullivan when the feisty host of *The Tonight Show* warned him just hours before the Stone's appearance, "Either that song goes or you go!" The title had for one evening been changed to "Let's Spend *Some Time* Together."

In January 1967 Decca released Marianne's fourth studio album. There had been one pop predecessor, two folk: now, *Love In A Mist*, with its cover-shot of Marianne in a shimmering shirt and Elvis Presley tie, was a juxtaposition of both genres, the type of album the record company had wanted to bring out in the first place. It opens with "Yesterday", whence the mood changes slightly with the sultry but sweet "You Can't Go Where The Roses Go", the first of two Jackie DeShannon numbers—the second, "With You In Mind", was written not for Marianne but for Joe and Eddie, a popular American gospel duo whose partnership had ended tragically the previous August, when Joe Gilbert had died in a car crash. There were two songs by Donovan—"Good Guy", and "Hampstead Incident", an oddity from his *Mellow Yellow* album. Marianne performs it as "In The Night Time". There are three numbers from the pen of Tim Hardin (1941-80), one of her favorite songwriters who died of a heroin overdose on her birthday: "Hang Onto A Dream", "Don't Make Promises" and a near-definitive version of the much more celebrated "Reason To Believe". In 1979 Marianne recorded one of his last songs, "Brain Drain", for her *Broken English* album. A brave move for her now was to include "I Have A Love", from *West Side Story*. This she sings beautifully, her voice tremendously moving while mounting from contralto to mezzo-soprano with comparative ease, ending with an astonishing Top C! There is "Young Girl Blues", which deals albeit surreptitiously with the then taboo subject of female masturbation. Perhaps the only poor track here is "Our Love Is Gone", from the pen of Sandie Shaw's anchorman, Chris Andrews.

Coinciding with the album and adhering to a regular Faithfull theme of infidelity, Decca released a single, "Is This What I Get For Loving You?"—an absolute corker of a song from the Spector-Goffin-King partnership which had been introduced by the Ronettes in 1965, and covered by Melinda Marx, daughter of comic Groucho. Neither version holds a candle to Marianne's. Both the single and the album showed tremendous potential, and almost certainly would have charted—"Is This What I Get For Loving You?" stalled at Number 43—had Marianne been available to promote it. Two things prevented this: her stage debut, and the controversy which unfolded that spring. Marianne also recorded Billie Holiday's classic "Some Other Spring", a delightful piece which was only released in the USA on the *Faithfull Forever* compilation.

The media, merely titillated by the events in San Remo, had an absolute field-day not long afterwards when the so-called "Redlands Bust" took place at Keith Richard's thatched, moated property near Chichester, in West Sussex.

The whole exercise appears to have been a deliberate set-up: a national newspaper seeking revenge because someone whose reputation it had attempted to sully fought back—aided by the ones Marianne scathingly referred to as "these little men in Whitehall....perverse aficionados of the Rolling Stones, in the same way the censors at the Vatican are forced to become connoisseurs of pornography and blasphemy." Those who looked down their noses at rock stars in general imagined non-stop, drugs and drink-fueled orgies taking places behind the security-protected facades of superstar flats and mansions. Mick Jagger was perceived as some kind of latter day anti-Christ, and clearly needed to be put in his place along with the other members of this "group from hell". In targeting Jagger, the *News Of The World* had however picked on the wrong person, though in the end his victory would be decidedly pyrrhic.

What set the ball rolling was a feature in the *News Of The World* accusing Jagger of taking benzadrine during a visit to Blaizes nightclub, in Kensington, and then taking two girls back to Harley House to smoke marijuana. Jagger reacted by serving the paper with a writ, threatening to sue them unless they printed a retraction. None was forthcoming. According to Marianne, the editor and his staff—the only ones aware of the writ—got in touch with MI5 and between them elected to set Mick Jagger up for an almighty fall. In fact, Jagger himself announced that he was taking action against the *News Of The World* on 5 February, when the Stones appeared on television's *The Eamon Andrews Show*. It is now known that whoever set them up flew in a notorious drugs dealer from California—27-year-old David Sniderman (aka David Jove, "The Acid King") whose speciality was "White Lightning", a powerful LSD-type narcotic. Sniderman turned up at the flat of the Stones' friend, Robert Fraser, with a large stash of the drug. Fraser (1937-86), nicknamed "Groovy Bob", ran a famous gallery in Duke Street. Over the years he would be largely responsible for introducing Britain to the works of Andy Warhol, Gilbert and George, and Jim Dine—an exhibition of the latter's paintings, deemed obscene, saw Fraser prosecuted in 1966. A promiscuous homosexual, one of his proudest boasts was that, during a trip to Africa, he had become the lover of the young Idi Amin. Marianne claimed that she was the one who suggested that everyone convene at Redlands at the weekend: herself, Jagger and Keith Richards, Fraser and his Moroccan houseboy Mohammed Jajaj, a friend named Christopher Gibbs, the flower-child socialite Nicky Kramer—and Sniderman, who supplied the "sacrament" early the next morning. George and Patti Harrison *were* at the house, but left an hour or so before the police arrived. Also present was the photographer Michael Cooper, who designed the covers for the Beatles' *Sergeant Pepper's* and the Stones *Satanic Majesties* albums.

Nineteen police officers turned up at Redlands at around 5.30 pm that same day, 11 February, with a search warrant. Contrary to some press reports they did not "storm" the property—they knocked on the front door, and Keith Richards let them in. Only then did things turn a little stroppy, when the police segregated the occupants into two groups—pop stars and their friends in one, the household staff in another—before conducting a thorough search. Everyone at Redlands had spent the day rambling through the woods surrounding the house, and getting high on marijuana, before heading for a nearby beach. Marianne, whose clothes and hair had ended up spattered with mud, had just taken a bath and was wearing nothing but an orange fur rug— according to a fabricated story which has entered into folk legend and will follow her until the end of her days, when she was apprehended, Mick Jagger was eating a Mars bar out of her vagina. Much was also made of the fact that Christopher Gibbs and Robert Fraser were gay.

Obviously, whoever had set the ball rolling for this fiasco was intent on humiliating everyone involved. The police found tablets in Jagger's jacket pocket which, to protect Marianne, he said were his—though these contained a minuscule amount of speed, these were her perfectly legal (at least in Italy) seasickness pills, prescribed by a doctor when she and Jagger had gone yachting after the San Remo Festival. More seriously they found 24 stacks of heroin in a pillbox belonging to Robert Fraser. Nicky Kramer, with his long blond hair, pancake make-up, and multicoloured pyjamas, was initially mistaken for a woman—a policewoman apparently only discovered that he was a man when she frisked him. The *Times*, when reporting the incident described him as "an exotic from Chelsea". The task of searching Marianne, the only woman at the party and referred to by the press as "Miss X" until later in the proceedings when they learned her identity, was given to D C Fuller, one of three policewomen who attended the bust. She wanted to give Marianne a "thorough examination" in one of the bedrooms rather than on the stairs where she had been apprehended. Having nothing to hide, Marianne let the rug drop to the floor and gave everyone an eyeful. "I couldn't help myself. I've always been an incorrigible exhibitionist," she recalled, "It was the gulf between us, on acid, and them with their notepads that made it seem so hilarious at the time. I certainly got paid back in spades."

David Sniderman, the alleged orchestrator of all this, was also searched by the police, who found a large number of "incredibly lumpy packages" in his attaché case. These were left unopened when he explained that they contained unexposed films which would be ruined if the police removed their tin-foil covering. That same day, he disappeared, and soon afterwards flew back to Los Angeles.

Though aware of the details of the raid, the press were prohibited from revealing names for fear of litigation. The banner headline across the front page of the *New Of The World* read, "Drugs Squad Raids Pop Stars Party" but did not give much away—other than that "several stars, at least three of them nationally known" had been involved, and that the raid had taken place "at a secluded country house near the South coast." In the wake of this report, the *Daily Express* declared, "A village was talking yesterday about the night a drugs squad raided Rolling Stone Keith Richards' country hideaway." It was not until 18 March that the *Daily Mirror* revealed that Jagger and Richards, along with David Sniderman and Robert Fraser, had been arraigned to appear before a Chichester magistrate "some time in May" to face drugs charges.

Thus far Marianne's name had not been mentioned in connection the scandal: she was able to get along with her career almost as if nothing had happened. She had acquired her Equity card and bagged the part of Irina Prozonova in the Royal Court Theatre's production of Chekhov's *The Three Sisters*—an excellent debut for a young woman who had always dreamed of becoming an actress, but forced by fate to accept what she may have regarded as second-best, a pop career which appeared to be now on the wane. Her co-stars were Glenda Jackson and Avril Elgar. Marianne had been earning in excess of £300 for a single concert, but did not mind in the least her salary dropping to just £30 a week because she was doing something she was truly happy with.

Rehearsals for the play began in mid-February, and early in March, Marianne took advantage of a long weekend break to jet off to Morocco with Brian Jones and Anita Pallenberg. Mick Jagger, Keith Richards, and most of those who had been at Redlands at the time of the bust were already there to evade the media intrusion. Jones had emerged from a spell in nursing home, having suffered from pneumonia and drugs-induced exhaustion. Though no one outside his inner circle was aware of the fact, he had entered the final phase of his short life and was fading fast. At some stage during the trip—trip being the operative word, for all three were high much of the time—Jones is reported to have beaten up Pallenberg and, whilst attacking her a second time to have broken his arm. The incident brought their stormy relationship to an end, and she had taken up with Keith Richards. In Tangier, the Stones' party stayed at the plush El Minzah Hotel, where the men were courted by photographer Cecil Beaton, an undisputed connoisseur of young men who set his sights on Jagger and Richards. During the sessions next to the pool which resulted in some quite stunning shots, Jagger managed to keep on his grubby tee-shirt, but Beaton persuaded Richards to go topless. The picture of Beaton in excruciatingly tight shorts, snapping away at the prostrate guitarist and almost allowing us to read his thoughts—"Ah, if only!"—remains a potent exercise in inadvertent homoeroticism.

One evening, so the story goes, the Stones and their party visited a restaurant where a young man was busking—the then completely unknown Nick Drake, who would remain virtually so until being rediscovered several years after his death in 1974. In 2008, Marianne paid tribute to arguably Britain's greatest ever *chansonnier* by including one of his favourite songs, Jackson Franck's world-weary "Kimbie"—which Drake performed in Tangier—on her *Easy Come, Easy Go* album.

The Three Sisters opened at the end of April, with more emphasis placed on Marianne than on her co-stars—the reason having less to do with her acting abilities than with Mick Jagger turning up at the theatre each evening, usually to catch the last act before whisking Marianne off to some nightclub or party. Glenda Jackson is said to have been annoyed to discover, on opening night, not the regular bunch of flowers from Jagger, but a six-foot orange tree!

Marianne received pretty good reviews for her performance. *Plays & Players'* David Benedictus, ironically writing on the eve of the Redlands trial, called her, "A symbol of radiance and innocence, a rubbing post for our itchy souls." Worrying over the impending drama did however prove too much for her when, during the final week of the production, she collapsed on stage and had to be replaced for the rest of the run by an understudy—resulting in a drop in ticket sales.

During the trial, "Miss X" was perceived as the victim, the convent-educated teenager led astray by a bunch of demonic rockers. "Mick was a filthy, deprived maniac and I was the Dickensian innocent caught up in the monster's clutches," Marianne observed. Jagger and Richards were brought before the soon to retire Justice Leslie Block on 10 May, where the charges were read out and the pair released on £100 bail. Their defence QC was one of the country's best: Michael Havers, father of actor Nigel, and later Attorney General. The Jagger-Richards case would be the first of three infamous miscarriages of justice successfully defended by him, the others being the Maguire Seven and the Guildford Four. Havers put in a plea that they should be tried separately from Robert Fraser, his theory being that Fraser's much more serious charge of heroin possession might affect their lesser charge of amphetamine possession. That same day, in what was subsequently revealed to have been another set-up, Brian Jones was arrested in the flat he had just moved into. The arresting officer, DS Norman Pilcher, claimed to have found hashish in a drawer, whilst Jones argued that this had been left there by the previous tenant. Almost certainly this was planted by a dealer hired by Pilcher. In 1973, he would be charged with perverting the course of justice, and jailed for four years.

The trials took place on 27 and 28 June, with all three men detained in custody until sentencing had taken place on the 29th. Jagger and Richards' court appearances, if anything, adhered them to much of the public who until now had regarded them with disdain: not the scruffy rockers of legend, but two well-dressed, well-mannered young men. Marianne stayed away from Jagger's trial, but turned up for Richards and Fraser's hearing. It must have been torture for her, hearing prosecutor Michael Morris persistently referring to "Miss X in the fur rug", whilst asking the court not to be prejudiced towards her, whoever she was, because *she* was not to blame for what had happened. By now, everyone in the room knew who Miss X was, including the press, but they were prohibited from revealing this just yet in case Jagger and Richards were cleared. The actual rug was submitted as evidence—to prove that it had been large enough to cover Miss X's naked body, and that she had not wrapped herself in it purely as an act of titillation. Miss X was described by DC Rosemary Slade, as having been "in a merry mood and one of vague concern" when apprehended on the stairs at Redlands. The fictitious "Mars bar story", not mentioned in court or by the media (who in 1967 would never have been permitted to use words like "vagina" and "cunnilingus") had already entered pop lore, almost certainly courtesy of a downright spiteful policeman. Years later, Marianne would still be feeling understandably bitter, but not averse to injecting a little humour into the story:

> Mick retrieving a Mars bar from my vagina! It was far too jaded even for any of us to have conceived of. It's a dirty old man's fantasy, some old fart who goes to a dominatrix every afternoon to lick her boots and get spanked. A cop's idea of what people do on acid, for Christ's sake.

Yet it was Michael Havers himself who, perhaps unwittingly, levelled the gravest insult against Marianne when, in defence of "Miss X" being summoned to give evidence, he pronounced,

> Miss X is not on trial. She is a girl who remains technically anonymous, and I hope she will remain anonymous. She is described as a drug-taking nymphomaniac with no chance of saying anything in her defence. Do you expect me to force that girl to go into the witness to refute the allegations? I am not going to tear the blanket aside and subject her to laughter and scorn.

The repercussions over what Havers said tormented Marianne for years to come. That same evening, she was snapped on the grounds at Redland by a reporter who had been instructed to lay in wait, in the bushes, like a predator. She was clutching a newspaper, the headlines of which had been enhanced by the laboratory to read, "Naked Girl At Stones Party". Effectively, she had outed herself as

60

"Miss X". The following week, despite being edited by her friend Barry Fantoni, *Private Eye* ran the headline, "A Mars Bar That Fills The Gap".

The jury were out for mere minutes: though clearly there was no way these "reprobates" could get away with what they had supposedly done. Jagger and Richards were found guilty, and each given a three-month prison sentence. Both put in appeals. Robert Fraser was sentenced to six months hard labour at Wormwood Scrubs, an ordeal from which he would never recover. In 1969, addicted to heroin, he closed his gallery and left England to live in India with his mother. The episode also ended the Rolling Stones' tenure with Andrew Loog Oldham, who had stayed out of the country whilst his "boys" had been going through their trauma.

Some fans reacted as they might have, had Jagger and Richards died. Overnight vigils were held in Piccadilly Circus, while in New York hundreds protested their innocence outside the British Consulate. This resulted in their appeal being brought forward and personally heard by the Lord Chief Justice. The sentence against Richards was overturned, and Jagger's reduced to a conditional discharge. The tabloids had their say, but Jagger and Richards found themselves championed by an unlikely source, the *Times* William Rees-Mogg who on 1 July 1967 penned a defence (borrowing a quote from English satirist Alexander Pope) entitled, "Who Breaks A Butterfly On A Wheel?"

Basically, Rees-Mogg was demanding an equality in the law "in the conflict between the sound traditional values of Britain and the new hedonism," which would see the likes of Mick Jagger treated no differently than "any purely anonymous young man." He cited a hypothetical example: regarding the tablets found in Jagger's [sic] possession, should the Archbishop of Canterbury buy a proprietary brand of airsickness tablets at Rome airport and bring what was left of these into Britain, would he be guilty of the same crime as Jagger?" Rees-Mogg was of course missing the point entirely. Jagger was a cultural icon to whom millions of impressionable youngsters looked up to, not just in Britain but around the world. Therefore he could *not* expect to be granted the same treatment as a lesser mortal. *Had* he truly been guilty as charged, as opposed to being set up, then he had every right to be made an example of. And now, instead of being vilified, the Rolling Stones had been elevated to the status of national treasures—though Marianne would never live down her part in their ordeal.

With Glenda Jackson and Avril Elgar in *The Three Sisters*.

With Mick Jagger.

4: Counting Times That...

Comparisons may be made at this stage in Marianne's career with the great soprano, Maria Callas, whose amorous involvement with Greek shipping tycoon Aristotle Onassis virtually put paid to her glittering operatic career: the fact that, she was so obsessed with the high-life Onassis could offer her, despite her independent wealth, she was willing to let everything fall by the wayside for love. For a while after the Redlands bust, Marianne was no longer Marianne Faithfull the talented young singer. She was Mick Jagger's girlfriend, the former "Miss X" and his "bit on the side", the girl in the fur rug alleged to favour kinky sexual practices. Rarely has any artiste been treated so shabbily and been shown such unwarranted disrespect by the media.

This negative publicity—the fact that no matter what happened, so long as she stayed with Jagger, Marianne would be walking in the shadow of his sun—began affecting their relationship. Talent had little to do with it, for nothing could ever alter the fact that Jagger would always be the bigger star. Marianne's success on the stage proved, if proof was required, that she had a great deal more to offer the entertainment world than her current position as consort to the Prince of Pop, and she was starting to regret cutting back on the music career she had been willing to abandon. There was also the rumour that Jagger was thinking of popping the question, and that they would marry as soon as Marianne acquired a divorce from John Dunbar. He, however, was interested in a reconciliation so that they could be a family again. Marianne had been granted custody of

Nicholas, who had run away from Harley House on at least one occasion in an attempt to find his father, only to end up having Marianne collect him from the nearest police station.

During the summer of 1967, Jagger and Marianne moved out of Harley House and into a large, rented property in Cheyne Walk, Chelsea—Keith Richards and Anita Pallenberg lived just down the road. Jagger also forked out £25,000 for Stargroves, a ten-bedroomed mansion near Newbury in Berkshire —later described by a local newspaper as "Jagger's Folly" because the couple only spent the odd weekend here. Whether Jagger was faithful to her is not known, but unlikely: Marianne was still something of a loose cannon, and confessed to having almost become Jimi Hendrix's lover at around this time. She had first met rock's wildest wild man—described by her as "a Tantric vision in fashionable rushed velvet pants and ruffled shirt" at London's Seven-and-a-Half Club, and rued not having grasped the opportunity to seduce him then. Now, after his performance at the Speakeasy, Hendrix swaggered over to Marianne and Jagger's table and made no secret of his hatred of Jagger, or the fact that he wanted her, pronouncing very loudly so that Jagger heard every word, "Come with me now, baby. Let's split! What are you doing with this jerk anyway?" Marianne's response was equally astonishing: "I wanted more than anything to go off with him....Mick would never have forgiven me."

On 25 June, the Rolling Stones and the Beatles joined forces when Mick Jagger, Brian Jones, Keith Richards and Marianne were asked to participate in *Our World*, a nineteen-nation protest against the Six

Day War, and featuring artistes as diverse as Maria Callas and Pablo Picasso. Watched by 400 million people in twenty-five countries, this was broadcast by satellite and the Beatles closed the proceedings with "All You Need Is Love"—the Stones' party are seen sitting cross-legged on the floor, gazing up at their "idols" with other fans, before joining in with the seemingly never-ending chorus. John Lennon and Paul McCartney returned the compliment by participating in the four-minute (before the advent of promo-videos) promotional film for the Stones' next single, the equally monotonous "We Love You", their last with Andrew Loog Oldham, and a thank-you to fans who had voiced their support after the Redlands bust. Jagger and Richards juxtaposed this event and its aftermath with Oscar Wilde's 1895 trial for indecency. In this psychedelic collage of clanking prison doors, rattling chains and frilly shirts, Jagger becomes Wilde, Richards is the Marquis of Queensbury, and the hapless Lord Alfred Douglas is portrayed by Marianne in a short brown wig. John Lennon is the judge, while Brian Jones hovers in the background—in the two brief close-ups he is completely out of it in a drugs-induced stupor, a clear indication of the tragedy around the corner. Off-camera was the equally spooked out Allen Ginsberg, "directing" the action with a Tibetan oracle ring. Oh dear! Later he would recall of the glamorous gathering, "They looked like little angels, like Botticelli Graces singing together for the first time." The "singing" was little more than a tuneless chant: "We don't care if you hound 'we' and lock the doors around 'we'....you'll never win 'we'." Then the historic farce draws to a close as

Marianne-Douglas presents her evidence to Judge Lennon—the orange fur rug she was wearing at Redlands, from under which *Jagger* emerges naked!

That August bank holiday Marianne travelled with the Rolling Stones (the Beatles were already there) to Bangor, North Wales, to attend one of the Maharishi Mahesh Yogi's transcendental meditation teach-ins. They were here when news came in of Brian Epstein's death. Marianne later said how appalled she had been by the attitude of the holy man scathingly referred to by *Private Eye* as "The Veririchi Lotsamoney Yogi Bear"—the Maharishi's theory being that, when a person "moves on", just as he no longer needs the family he left behind, so they will no longer need him. In *Memories, Dreams & Reflections* she claims that, during one of her frequent visits to his home, Epstein had asked her to marry him. "Not that he was exactly serious," she added, "But for a second I actually considered it." She also upheld the suicide theory, unlike some of those close to him who did not want to believe he had killed himself, simply because they were afraid of being implicated in his downfall. Comparing Epstein with Andrew Loog Oldham, she believed that whereas Oldham had embraced and enjoyed *his* demons, Epstein had allowed his to destroy him.

Marianne's success in *The Three Sisters* led to two film offers—one instantly forgettable, the other a classic. She wisely rejected the part of Dave Clark's girlfriend in *Catch Us If You Can*, declaring that it was not artistic enough. However, to turn down a supporting role in Ken Russell's adaptation of D H Lawrence's *Women In Love* was sheer folly: she would have appeared alongside a stellar cast, which included Oliver Reed, Alan Bates, and Glenda Jackson. It was suggested at the time, though not proved, that Marianne did not relish working with Jackson again after the latter's frosty reaction to Mick Jagger's orange tree gift when they had been doing the Chekhov play.

What Marianne *did* accept were roles in two films which were unbelievably tacky whilst clearly fitting into the "so-bad-it's-good" category: *I'll Never Forget Whats'is Name* and *Girl On A Motorcycle*. The tagline for the first film (in which she was seventh lead) read, "He smashed up his desk, gave up his wife, three mistresses, and went back to the simple life. Then his troubles *really* started!" The "he" is advertising executive Oliver Reed who, tired of his extremely successful life, throws a fit with boss Orson Welles, quits his job, and takes a position with an inconsequential literary magazine, only to be haunted by the demons from his past. That just about sums up the feeble plot—along with Marianne's distinction of being allowed to play the first character in a mainstream film to say the word "fuck", or in this instance, "fucking bastard". This was not the reason, however, for the film initially being refused a certificate for US release—but the implication (not actually shown on the screen) of oral sex between Reed and *Cathie Come Home* actress Carol White.

The second film, released the following year, saw Marianne sharing equal billing with French acting heartthrob Alain Delon. Based on a short story by André Pieyre Mandiargues, *La motocyclette* (the film's French title in the dubbed version), this one boasted a tag-line which had the detractors howling:

"This Girl Is A Wild Ride!" In some countries it was released as *Naked Under Leather*: the title courtesy of the leather body suit worn by Marianne in the film, under which she (or rather, her body stand-in) is naked. The storyline, tame today, was hugely controversial back then—Rebecca, a newly-married woman, deserts her new husband, mounts her bike, and rides all the way to her lover, Daniel, in Heidelberg. En-route she experiences psychedelic fantasies about her two relationships before coming to a sticky, if not unintentionally hilariously funny end—by which time we have lost all sympathy for her character, if indeed it was ever there in the first place. The "action" scenes, where we see Marianne riding her "black pimp" machine are dire beyond comprehension, and the soft-porn scenes little better. The film was directed by Jack Cardiff, a much better cinematographer (*Black Narcissus*, *The African Queen*) than he was a director. Even so, *Girl On A Motorcycle* was considered more than adequate fare for the Cannes Film Festival, but cancelled owing to the May 1968 student riots. It also has a fine soundtrack by Les Reed, who gave Engelbert Humperdinck and Tom Jones several Numbers Ones at around this time. Despite their on-screen chemistry, however, Marianne does not appear to have enjoyed working with Alain Delon, and accused him of being "sullen and difficult....a pompous git" when she turned down his amorous advances. Some years later, she would criticise him again—and some!—in her "Song For Nico".

In February 1968, Marianne did her "reputation" few favours by allowing herself to be interviewed by Michael Barrett, for the BBC's *Personal Choice* programme. Today, she would have handled the no nonsense Barrett with ease—back then, though opinionated, her fragility, mild-mannered approach and eagerness to respond to any question flung her way saw her putting her foot in it with every response. Foremost on Barrett's agenda was the topic of drugs, and once Marianne started on this there seemed to be no stopping her. Marijuana, she pronounced, was perfectly safe, and drugs were the doors of perception: "If LSD wasn't meant to have happened, it wouldn't have been invented. It's as important as Christianity—more important!" She also attacked the establishment—"the little men in their offices"—who she accused of dwelling in the past. She opined:

> We're just blinded by their past. We're seeing walls that aren't even there any more, and it's just stupid. We're taking orders from a bunch of dead men, and it's insane....I know so many people who, before they took LSD, were such a *drag*. But they took LSD and they opened up!

When bringing up the topic of marriage, Barrett was hinting that, at the very least, Marianne was a serial adulteress, and she did not disappoint, though the answer was short and sharp: "For some people, marriage may be very groovy. For me, it wasn't."

And, Barrett finally wanted to know, how would her little son be affected by all of this. Marianne merely shrugged her shoulders and responded, "He's going to *have* to make it. It will throw him on his feet!"

The press lampooned Marianne, and attacked her for her relaxed attitude towards drugs, and for "living in sin" though nothing prepared her for what happened next. On 31 March, she returned to the Royal Court Theatre to play Florence Nightingale in Edward Bond's *Early Morning*. One of the most controversial playwrights of his day, Bond had hit the headlines a few years earlier with his first work, *The Pope's Wedding*, in which a baby is stoned to death in its pram. The new play was his take on Victorian England where Queen Victoria (Moira Redmond) has a lesbian affair with Florence Nightingale, the royal princes are conjoined twins, and Disraeli and Prince Albert are terrorists. Thrown into the mix was a little cannibalism, and the production ends with everyone falling off the cliffs at Beachy Head!

Despite heckling from a handful of moralists, the first performance saw the cast receiving a standing ovation. The next morning, however, the theatre manager received a visit from the police, who threatened him with an injunction unless he closed the production. He agreed to do this, but such were the protests from the actors that he consented to the play finishing its run. It finally closed when ticket sales slumped after London's top theatre critic, Harold Hobson, denounced it as, "Like a nightmare dreamed up by an overheated child, an unspeakably horrible experience." Marianne's nastier detractors among the press declared her a national pariah, and their spite escalated in the July when Mick Jagger told reporters outside the house in Cheyne Walk that she was pregnant. Then, in one fell swoop he turned her into "pop depravity's sacrificial lamb" by adding, "There'll probably be another three children. As for marriage, I can't see that happening. We don't believe in it!" What is interesting is that the media did not make as much fuss over Keith Richards and Anita Pallenberg's "common-law" status: between now and going their separate ways in 1979, the couple would have three children.

Jagger's statement raised the hackles of Warwickshire housewife Mary Whitehouse, the self-appointed clean-up campaigner. In September, they clashed swords on television's *The David Frost Show*, a hilariously amusing exercise with neither side claiming victory. Whitehouse regarded Jagger as a symbol of depravity amongst the nation's youth—in his opinion, *she* was just another old fuddy-duddy with nothing better to do than tell other people how to live their lives. The one who emerged from the debacle truly besmirched was Marianne. Rock stars who bedded different girls every night on the tour circuit were "lucky guys" while the girls they bedded were "sluts". There had been hate-mail after the Redlands bust, but nothing like this—pleas for Marianne to kill herself and her unborn baby, denunciations from pulpits—including one from the Archbishop of Canterbury—and vile attacks from the tabloids. She evaded much of this backlash by moving to Ireland with Nicholas and Eva, renting a secluded house in Galway. Jagger, who had just begun shooting his first feature film, *Performance*, visited whenever he could.

If he was hoping to salvage his and Marianne's reputation, his choice of role could not have been more inappropriate. *Performance*, directed by Nicolas Roeg, was a deeply unpleasant film, with its

72

over-emphasis on homophobia, drug abuse, sexual sadism, mysogyny, and East End gangs, and with personal appearances by real-life hoodlums such as John Binden. Much-feared mobster David Litvinoff was hired as the film's "criminal adviser" to ensure that the violence was not underplayed. "They were making a film of what the public imagined our lives to be," Marianne observed. The censor considered it so bad that it took two years for the distributor to acquire a certificate for its release, though it is now regarded as a cult movie. Marianne should have been playing Jagger's girlfriend, but owing to her pregnancy had to back out—she was replaced by Anita Pallenberg, with whom Marianne said Jagger had an affair, but which Pallenberg has always denied. The part of the psychotic gangster who, after a failed heist, lies low at a guest-house run by faded rock star Turner (Jagger) should have been played by Marlon Brando, but when he backed out it was given to James Fox.

During breaks in the shooting schedule, Jagger supervised a redecoration programme at Cheyne Walk, which included building a nursery. Marianne had fallen ill with anaemia, and in the middle of November returned to London, where Eva found her a room at a nursing home in St John's Wood. On 22 November, seven months into her term, she went into premature labour and was delivered of a stillborn daughter, which she named Corrina. The death of her baby was the beginning of the end, so far as her relationship with Jagger was concerned.

Just weeks after her loss, Marianne participated in the Rolling Stones' latest costly folly—*Rock & Roll*

Circus, a £50,000-plus big-top special which saw world famous rock stars sharing the bill with fire-eaters, contortionists, trapeze artistes and clowns. Directed by Michael Lindsay-Hogg, the baronet son of American actress Geraldine Fitzgerald, the film which featured Brian Jones' last public performance began shooting on 11 December 1968. At their own expense, the Stones ferried over 800 guests, mostly in chauffeur-driven taxis, to the big top which had been constructed on a Wembley sound-stage. The musical specialities included The Who, Jethro Tull, Eric Clapton, Anita Pallenberg, John Lennon—and Yoko Ono, who had lost her own baby the day before Marianne. The audience were supplied with brightly-coloured ponchos and sou'westers. Filming started off well enough. Introduced by drummer Charlie Watts, Marianne performed Spector-Goffin-King's "Something Better", a new song, sitting in the middle of the circus ring, wearing a full-length black crepe gown. Her voice had changed—drugs and cigarettes had given it a deeper, darker sound, but still one of exceptional quality. From this stage in the shooting, however, there were any number of production problems—amplifiers not working, cameras breaking down—so that by the time the Stones got around to their set they gave a lacklustre performance. This they put down to the fact that, since the Redlands bust, they had given few live shows. When Mick Jagger viewed the edited footage, he was so disappointed that he petitioned the Stone's manager, Allen Klein, to cancel the film's release. This brought a storm of protests from The Who, who had been in fine fettle: there was even talk of Klein re-editing the as *The Who's Rock*

& Roll Circus—Featuring The Rolling Stones. Eventually, it was assigned to a vault from which it did not emerge until 2004.

In February 1969, Marianne realized her dream of working with Nicol Williamson when Tony Richardson cast her as Ophelia in his avante-garde production of *Hamlet*: his production notes describe the Prince of Denmark as "an anti-establishment dropout" and Ophelia as "sensual, but barking mad". Also in the cast were Judy Parfitt, Gordon Jackson and Anthony Hopkins. The play opened at London's Roundhouse, and one of the performances was filmed as an educational film for schools, though it went on general release during the summer. *Time* magazine described Marianne's interpretation as, "Remarkably affecting....ethereal, vulnerable, purer than the infancy of youth." She later confessed to having an affair with Williamson—and to adding a little Method acting to Ophelia's mad scene by taking a jack of heroin shortly before going on stage. "I *am* Ophelia," she told one reporter, "I *know* what it's like to be mad!"

Marianne had been away from the recording scene for two years—a long time for a Sixties pop star—and when she gave Decca an inkling that she was in no hurry to cut new material, they released a compilation of her work as part of their popular *World of....* series. *The World Of Marianne Faithfull* included her chart A-sides, and other favourites including "Scarborough Fair" and "Go Away From My World". One single emerged at this time: "Something Better", from the recent Rolling Stones film, backed with "Sister Morphine". Marianne had written the lyrics to this latter song, during a visit to

75

Rome, and Jagger had supplied the music—on the original label it is wrongly accredited to Jagger and Richards, an error which was later rectified. For some time, Marianne had considered her singing career to be at a dead end. "Sister Morphine", she said, and not "Something Better" should have been the key to her resurrection—an attempt "to make art out of a pop song". Neither was the song about her, as many would later assume when the Rolling Stones revived it for their *Sticky Fingers* album. The lyrics tell the story of a man close to death after being injured in a car crash. All he wants is for his suffering to end, so he tells his nurse, "Please, Sister Morphine, turn my nightmares into dreams." On the Continent, such themes had been popular since the turn of the century. The great French singer, Damia, whose "Sombre dimanche" Marianne later recorded, had a huge hit with a similiar song, "J'ai le cafard", back in 1926. Marianne's record was pressed and released, but apparently with none of the Decca executives listening to the B-side until the first batches were on their way out of the factory. Only five-hundred copies slipped though the net, resulting in the single becoming an immensely sought after collectors' item.

The banning of "Sister Morphine", Marianne said, almost completed the disintegration of her relationship with Mick Jagger: he had fought tooth and nail with the Decca top brass over the cover of the Stones' *Beggars Banquet* album—this depicted a filthy toilet above which was scribbled all manner of graffiti—yet he had not used any of his power to prevent them from giving the thumbs-down to her best song in years. Now it is a classic, and regularly features in hit compilations concerts. On her version of the song, Marianne is accompanied by an eclectic group of musicians: Jagger on acoustic guitar, Charlie Watts on drums, Ry Cooder on slide, and producer Jack Nitzche on piano. Performed in a strident monotone half an octave lower than the fans were used to hearing, "Sister Morphine" may be regarded as Marianne's first work as a *sprechsinger*, a sign of great things to come—though between it and her bounce back to glory, a few years later, she would be dragged to hell and back.

With Alain Delon.

5: In My Time Of Sorrow

On 29 May 1969, Marianne and Mick Jagger hit the headlines again for all the wrong reasons, this time following a drugs bust the previous afternoon at Cheyne Walk. Whether this one was a set-up, like the last, is unclear: all that the police found was a small stash of cannabis, still enough for the couple to be whisked off to Chelsea Police Station and charged with possession.

It could have been worse. Since losing her baby, Marianne had taken up stronger substances. Along with Keith Richards and Anita Pallenberg she had begun "chasing the dragon"—smoking heroin—and was also cheating on Jagger with her dealer and Stones dogsbody "Spanish Tony" Sanchez. Like several of the men in her life, Marianne had a low opinion of this one, who would himself succumb to a heroin overdose: "He was a dreadful person. He was a low-life, a small-time spiv....completely hung up on his own particular sickness." Which begs the question—why bother with him in the first place? The answer to this was, with little money coming in now that her pop career appeared to have folded, she needed Spanish Tony to feed her habit. In his book, *Up And Down With The Rolling Stones*, Sanchez claims that Marianne sought him out on two occasions when she was at her lowest ebb: when she first realised that there would be no future with John Dunbar, and now, during the run-up to her break-up with Jagger.

This time the fans were well aware of what had happened: hundreds of them mobbed the couple outside Marlborough Magistrates Court. Jagger took advantage of the situation, announcing after the brief hearing (which saw the case adjourned until later in the summer), that this time, *he* had been "nabbed" by Tony Richardson—to play the part of Antipodean outlaw and folk hero Ned Kelly, hanged for murder in 1880. The film was to be shot on location in Australia and Marianne, he added, would be playing Kelly's sister, Maggie. What he was perhaps unaware of was that she had accepted the part in the hope that the three-month hiatus from the Rolling Stones and the heavy drugs scene might rebuilt their fractured relationship. She was also aware that Richardson was in love with Jagger, who had neither concealed his bisexuality nor refrained from sleeping with other men even when she was around. *Ned Kelly* attracted much adverse criticism, not least of all because Jagger was not a member of Australian Equity, and because he made no effort to affect an Australian accent. There were complaints from Kelly's descendants because Richardson had elected to film in New South Wales, rather than in Victoria, where most of the key events in his life had taken place. Not surprisingly, the film flopped at the box-office, and the world would have to wait until 2003 before seeing the definitive portrayal of Kelly, by Heath Ledger. Such was her infatuation with Jagger that Marianne turned down an offer to play Ophelia on Broadway to be with him. Had she flown East instead of West, things would have turned out less tragically than they did.

Meanwhile, Marianne was becoming increasingly concerned about Brian Jones' rapidly failing health. His drug intake had increased to the extent that he could barely function—and the other Stones wanted shot of him because he was becoming a liability. They got their wish on 9 June, when he left the group—one may not be sure whether by choice or not. Within days he was rumoured to be putting together a new band, though everyone knew that this would never happen because of his permanently addled state of mind. Marianne's latest fad was *I Ching*, an ancient Chinese practice of divination which involves tossing yarrow sticks or coins and then consulting a book of hexagrams. Marianne tossed her coins, and they concluded that Jones would die by water. Towards the end of June, she and Mick Jagger visited him at Redlands, where he was staying with Keith Richards and Anita Pallenberg. His split from the Stones had not affected his friendship with Richards, though an argument did ensue between Jones and Jagger, which resulted in the two men going outside for a punch-up which resulted in them falling into the moat. Marianne at once assumed that this was the *I Ching* prophesy coming partly true, and that she had misinterpreted the message from the coins. Then during the early hours of 3 July, Jones' body was found at the bottom of the pool at Cotchford Farm, his West Sussex retreat since November 1968—formerly the home of children's author A A Milne.

Brian Jones was just 27, and is listed among the "Twenty-Seven Club"—the blues and rock stars and actors who have died at that age, mostly as a result of self-destruction: Jimi Hendrix, Robert Johnson, Janis Joplin, Amy Winehouse, Kurt Cobain and Jim Morrison are the most famous casualties. The riddle of Jones' death may never be solved. His Swedish girlfriend Anna Wohlin claimed that he had a pulse, after being pulled out of the water. What is certain is that the paramedics, arriving soon afterwards, pronounced him dead at the scene. The coroner delivered a verdict of death by misadventure, and in his report revealed that Jones' heart and liver were greatly enlarged owing to alcohol and drug abuse. As with many deaths when the victim is young and good-looking, there were suspicions of suicide and foul play. One theory was that Jones killed himself because the Stones no longer felt that they had any use for him. "One of the things that keeps you alive when you're on the skids is that people care what happens to you," Marianne opined 25 years later, adding that in this respect, Jones had almost been like her twin, "It's your life thread, and with Brian nobody really cared any more. His fate could easily have been mine." Then, in 1999, Anna Wohlin claimed she had not been at the scene and that Jones had been murdered by Frank Thorogood, a builder working at Cotchford Farm who we do know was the last person to see him alive. Thorogood is said to have confessed to the killing on his deathbed, to Stones driver Tom Keylock—who later denied that any such confession having taken place.

The Stones had arranged a free open-air concert in Hyde Park, to be held on 25 July to introduce Jones' replacement, Mick Taylor. Now, it would serve as a tribute to the dead guitarist. Many fans deemed it the most underwhelming show of their career, and the "poncing and poovery" to have been in bad taste bearing in mind that one of the group's founding members was still lying on a mortuary slab—the victim, it was rumoured, of a suicide brought about by his being dumped. 250,000 fans turned up for the

81

event, which was filmed. Mick Jagger pranced on to the stage, wearing full make-up and a short white smock-dress over white baggy trousers. Behind him, a large colour photograph of Brian Jones surveyed the sea of faces as Jagger recited his "eulogy"—several stanzas of Shelley's "Adonais", written as a tribute to his poet friend, John Keats. "Peace, peace!" he pronounced, to loud guffaws from the audience, "He is not dead, he doth not sleep! He hath awakened from the dream of life!" Marianne, also dressed in white and with Nicholas on her knee, was sitting in the wings: as a form of penance she had cut her hair short—not just in mourning for Jones, but for the death of her marriage to John Dunbar. That morning, both had filed for divorce, Dunbar citing Jagger as co-respondent.

If Marianne was hoping for a life of domestic bliss with Jagger now that her marriage was over, she had another think coming. That evening, after the concert, while she was driven home to Cheyne Walk, Jagger headed off with Marsha Hunt, who he had been seeing for a while. Eight months younger than Marianne, married to the Soft Machine's Mike Ratledge, *and* four months pregnant with Jagger's child (their daughter, Karis, was born that November) the Philadelphia-born actress-singer had recently appeared in the London stage version of *Hair*. "Brown Sugar", the opening track of the Rolling Stones' *Sticky Fingers* album, would be about her. Whether Marianne knew about Jagger's affair with Hunt, or if she even cared, is not known. She certainly had nothing to reproach him for as she was still seeing Tony Sanchez. On the morning of 6

July, Jagger's car collected Marianne from Cheyne Walk, and they drove to Heathrow. Their press office announced that, much as they loathed having to miss Brian Jones' funeral, they had received word from the *Ned Kelly* production company that unless they turned up on the set on the 9th—the actual day of the funeral—they would be sued for breach of contract. This was not true. The Stones manager, Allein Klein, wanted Jagger out of the way to avoid the media circus if he attended the ceremony.

A few days before embarking on the long flight—36 hours in those days, including stopovers—Marianne visited her doctor and asked him for something to settle her nerves and help her through her grieving for Brian Jones: she had given Jagger her word that she would not be using heroin while in Australia. The doctor prescribed a three-month supply of Tuinal. A combination of secobarbital and amobarbital sodiums), this had been introduced several decades earlier as a sedative, though by the Sixties it was widely sold as a recreational drug, nicknamed "Christmas Trees" on account of the multicoloured capsules. Marianne is said to have taken fifteen while on the plane, to help her sleep. When she and Jagger arrived at Sydney's Kingsford Smith Airport they were jostled by reporters—some had seen newspaper photographs of Jagger at the Hyde Park concert, "looking like a tart", and wanted to know what right such a man had to be playing one of their greatest national heroes. Jagger bluffed his way through the press-conference, while Marianne clung to his arm, her obvious exhaustion put down to jet-lag.

The couple's reputation had preceded them. At the

airport they were questioned for thirty minutes by customs officers. It is quite likely that they were searched—if so the officers would have been shown evidence that Marianne had been *legally* prescribed the Tuinal by her doctor. They were then allowed to proceed with their journey, first to Ajaz Bay where the locations for *Ned Kelly* were scheduled to begin shooting the next day, then to the Chevron Hotel. What happened next in the plush suite on the 45th floor is unclear. Jagger is said to have got into bed and fallen asleep at once, whilst Marianne ordered a mug of hot chocolate from room service—an odd choice, considering the time of year. A few hours later she was rushed by ambulance to St Vincent's Hospital. Jagger had awoken suddenly and found Marianne lying unconscious next to him, and seen the empty Tuinal bottle on the bedside cabinet. He had called the downstairs desk, and the receptionist had contacted the hotel's on-call doctor before alerting the press. By the time Jagger arrived at the hospital, the place was swarming with reporters. Jagger, backed up by a hospital spokeswoman, denied that Marianne had taken an overdose, adding that she was suffering from no more than extreme exhaustion after the long flight. The papers believed differently, the *Sydney Sunday Mirror* leading the onslaught with the headline, "Drug Squad At Hospital", whilst other tabloids dismissed the exhaustion theory and began speculating over what she had overdosed on—moreover, who had supplied her with the near-fatal drugs. Jagger was obviously a suspect—and as had initially happened with the Redlands bust, Marianne was perceived as the innocent victim of rock star skullduggery.

The doctors at St Vincent's never worked out how many Tuinal Marianne had taken—she said 150, forgetting those she had taken on the plane. Given the strength of the drug, it seems unlikely that she swallowed so many, otherwise she would have been dead before reaching the hospital. Even so, she remained in a coma for six days, while drug-squad officers hung around, waiting for her to come to. Mick Jagger contacted Eva Faithfull, who took the next flight out to Sydney—her first act once she arrived was to contact a Catholic priest, who administered Last Rites. When one Australian newspaper reported that Marianne had suffered brain damage and was close to death, the editor of the *Times* in London commissioned an obituary. Mick Jagger spent as much time at her bedside as he could—this time the film company were genuinely threatening him with breach of contract, should he not turn up on the set for whatever reason. A press photographer, disguised as a doctor, sneaked into Marianne's room: within hours, her "deathbed" picture was wired around the world. Many newspapers included it on their front pages, next to photographs of Brian Jones' funeral. Jones had reputedly been buried twelve-feet deep to deter trophy hunters, in a casket provided by Bob Dylan. Of the Rolling Stones, only Bill Wyman and Charlie Watts attended the ceremony.

Once Marianne started to rally, Eva took over—even though Jagger, also spending a small fortune on overseas telephone calls to Marsha Hunt, was picking up the tab. She was transferred to Mount St Margaret's Hospital, a private clinic run by nuns. Here, with Eva sleeping in the next room, Marianne convalesced and received the psychiatric care Eva thought essential to her recovery. By 28 July she was well enough to give her first interviews: she told reporters how grateful she was to be still alive, and thanked fans from around the world for their messages of support. On the same day, she was interrogated by the police, who in an unprecedented move allowed the press to see their report. Marianne had not overdosed accidentally or otherwise on drugs, but on anti-depressants legally prescribed by her British doctor. She left the clinic on 6 August and, accompanied by Eva flew to Canberra, then to the location where Jagger was filming. Her part in *Ned Kelly* had been given to an unknown young actress, Diane Craig—in years to come she would become one of the queens of Australian soap operas with her portrayal of scheming matriarch Deborah McManus in *Out Of The Blue.*

Later, Marianne told friends (and explained most prosaically in her memoirs) of how after swallowing the Tuinal and immediately before going into her coma, she had met Brian Jones "on the other side". At first, she had considered jumping out of the hotel window, but had been unable to get this open. Then she had observed Jones, in the street below. This beckoning vision had enabled her to pass through the glass and join him in a landscape reminiscent of an Edmund Dulac illustration—they had eventually come to a cliff, but whereas Jones had disappeared over the edge, a sign that he had been truly dead, she had held back. "I heard a chorus of voices calling to me, but I wasn't ready just yet," she wrote, "I wanted to see some more." The next thing she remembered she said was gazing up at Jagger's face

86

—responding to his anguished declaration that he thought he had almost lost her with, "Wild horses wouldn't drag me away." It all sounds so terribly romantic, particularly as Jagger used the line—if indeed Marianne had pronounced it bearing in mind that some reports state her as incapable of speaking at all for several days, on account of the tubes which had caused her throat to swell—for the title of a song. "Wild Horses", co-written with Keith Richardsm, was given to Richards' friend, Gram Parsons, who recorded it with the Flying Burrito Brothers. The Stones themselves later included it on their *Sticky Fingers* album.

Marianne and Jagger had found themselves in an impossible to live with-to live without situation. In an act of self-loathing, she said, she had attempted suicide—partly to get away from him, partly to get her revenge on him. But for what? Theirs was a classic case of what was good for the goose was good for the gander. Jagger had a pregnant girlfriend at the other side of the world, and over the course of the next few months, like Marianne, would lose count of his amorous conquests. *Ned Kelly* wrapped and after a brief holiday in Indonesia the couple went their separate ways—Marianne to Yew Tree Cottage, Eva's property at Aldworth, near Reading, which Jagger had bought for his "mother-in-law", while Jagger flew with the Stones to Los Angeles, where after adding the finishing touches to their *Let It Bleed* album they prepared for their first major American tour in two years.

Marianne should have learned her lesson, yet no sooner had she returned to England than she was back to injecting heroin. In October, she flew to Los

Angeles, and was collected at the airport by Gram Parsons' road manager, Phil Kaufman. Over the next few weeks she saw more of Parsons and the Flying Burrito Brothers than she did her semi-estranged lover. Most evenings, she and Anita Pallenberg joined the group for a drive out to Joshua Tree—where in September 1973, Parsons' body would be subjected to al fresco cremation by Kaufman, allegedly adhering to the singer's last wishes—where they smoked pot, tripped, and gazed into the night sky in search of UFOs. Well aware that they would be incapable of resisting the groupies which always surrounded them when they were on the road, Marianne refused to accompany the Stones on tour. Flying back to England, she played Jagger at his own game, hooking up with Mario Schifano, an Italian painter and occasional film director with a history of drug abuse and, keeping things in the family so to speak, also a former lover of Anita Pallenberg. Marianne and Schifano were located early in December by the *Daily Mail*'s Rome correspondent—not living in some opulent mansion, but in a filthy apartment, reputedly putting Nicholas's health at risk. Marianne was understandably piqued at this intrusion into her privacy, and hit out, "The people in Britain imagine they have some form of right to me. They must realise that I'm not their property. What I do, say or think is absolutely no business of theirs. I'm happy, I'm penniless, and I'm going to start again from scratch. People can help by just forgetting me!"

Someone, almost certainly Eva Faithfull, got in touch with Jagger and begged him to come to Marianne's aid but right now he had problems of his own to deal with following the Stones free concert of 6 December at the Altamont Speedway, 50 miles east of San Francisco. Announced less than twenty-four hours in advance in response to media reports that the group were ripping fans off by charging too much for tickets, and badly organised, this saw them playing to an unruly 500,000-strong crowd, headlining a bill which included the Flying Burrito Brothers and Jefferson Airplane. Unable to organise security in time, the Stones hired the same "crack team" of Hell's Angels used to maintain order during recent concerts by the Grateful Dead, along with an "acid chemist" who provided refreshments for the artistes and their entourages—orange juice laced with LSD. Pandemonium erupted when the Hell's Angels began attacking over-excited fans with bicycle chains and baseball bats: during the Stones' set, a young man named Meredith Hunter was stabbed to death, and three more fans died in the early evening violence—two victims of a hit-and-run driver, the other drowning in an irrigation canal. Four women also went into premature labour and given birth.

In the wake of the most disastrous concert in rock history, Mick Jagger returned to England and lay low for a while at Cheyne Walk—Marsha Hunt moved in with him. In the middle of December he received a summons from Marlborough Magistrates Court: the hearing from the previous summer, twice postponed on account of Marianne's illness, had been rescheduled for 26 January 1970. Rather than discuss the matter with her over the phone, he flew to Rome on Christmas Eve, barged into the tawdry apartment she was sharing with Mario Schifano and announced that he would not be leaving without her. His caveman tactics worked: they flew back to London that same day. At the hearing, Jagger was fined £200 for possession, and ordered to pay costs. Marianne was acquitted. For a little while, the two attempted to rekindle their relationship, but by the end of March she was living with her mother at Yew Tree Cottage. For Marianne, the next few years would be arduous indeed.

As Ophelia, with Nicol Williamson.

Leaving the hospital in Australia.

6: The Most Of What Is Least

It is not the purpose of this book to delve too deeply into Marianne's so-called decline: others have done this, none less sparingly or more eloquently than Marianne herself:

> I knew that to destroy myself in [Mick's] eyes would be the worst torment I could inflict on him. Since he saw me as an extension of himself, it would be much the same as desecrating Mick....I self-destructed because that's the only way Mick would let me go.

According to Marianne, the Stones' management were starting to regard her as an embarrassment. The group had signed a new, $30 million contract with Atlantic Records and the company director, Ahmet Ertegun, did not want Mick Jagger to be involved with someone who was "out of control". Therefore in May 1970 she ended their relationship, and in October that year she and John Dunbar were divorced, the court granting them equal custody of Nicholas.

Lovers would come and go. For two years, anorexic and addicted to heroin, Marianne lived rough—in squats mostly. If Mick Jagger learned of her plight, so far as is known he never tried to rescue or help her. Most of her waking hours were spent occupying a wall next to a former bomb-site in Soho, waiting for the next fix. This she did with customary elegance and style, always wearing her best Ossie Clark dresses and other designer labels.

"The point was to be anonymous," she told the *Independent On Sunday*'s Fiona Sturgess in October 2004. "To have no address, and no phone number and have no one bothering me. For years I always had people looking at me, and I wanted it to stop."

A few people *did* recognise her, though. She was befriended by the painter Francis Bacon, who occasionally treated her to a meal at Wheelers restaurant, and now and then she returned to Yew Tree Cottage, where Eva had absolutely no idea of what was going on, otherwise one assumes she would have helped. Yet in her memoirs, Marianne seemingly has few regrets: "I had nothing, and even though nobody knew who I was, they still treated me like a human being, and for that I was eternally grateful."

Despite the obvious hardship, and between bouts of illness and one imagines near-despair, there were brief periods which saw Marianne almost getting back on track, personally and professionally. She became involved with Lord Paddy Rossmore, a relationship which the handsome young Irishman took seriously enough to propose marriage and pay for a course of treatment with a Harley street specialist. The union was scuppered by his elderly mother upon learning that her future daughter-in-law was a heroin addict. Unfazed, Marianne successfully auditioned for the part of Desdemona in the Birmingham production of Jack Good's *Catch My Soul: The Rock Othello*, starring Jerry Lee Lewis. Just days before the premiere she fell ill and was replaced by Dana Gillespie. In June 1970 she starred with Ian Ogilvy in *The Door of Opportunity*, an episode of the BBC's Somerset Maugham series.

This led to her being offered a part in Thomas Middleton's Jacobean drama, *Women, Beware, Women*. Again, she was forced to drop out because of illness. She also had to give up her role as Celimene in the Royal Lyceum Theatre's production of Moliere's *Le misanthrope* after badly twisting her ankle. Other setbacks are said to have been effected by the deaths of two rock legends—her friend of sorts and would-be lover Jimi Hendrix in the September, and Janis Joplin two weeks later.

That summer, Marianne had an affair with the French aristocrat, Jean de Breteuil (1949-71), who she later remembered as "a horrible guy, someone who had crawled out from under a stone." De Breteuil was the lover of her friend, Talitha Getty, and was known as "the dealer to the stars". It was he who may (but one of several theories) have supplied Jim Morrison with the drugs which killed him on 3 July 1971—an event which some say upset Marianne more than it normally would have done because this was two years to the day since Brian Jones' death. De Breteuil and Getty followed him to the grave soon afterwards, both victims of heroin overdoses. And, once again, Marianne was alone.

At around this time, Marianne appeared in *Lucifer Rising*, an experimental film shot on location in Egypt by the doyenne of psychedelic trash, Kenneth Anger. She played Lilith, and Anger cast Chris Jagger (younger brother of Mick) as Lucifer. "Like Cocteau, he's always had people he'd fucked or wanted to fuck in his films," she said. "Kenneth really wanted Mick....but Mick wouldn't do it, so Chris got the part." None of the actors were paid—it was as if Anger considered himself so eminent, that he could get almost anyone to work for him for nothing. Marianne had admired his *Scorpio Rising* (1964), an acknowledged classic featuring potent homoerotic imagery by way of a montage of Nazis, Hell's Angels, Jesus, sodomy, blow-jobs and Satanism. This one, in which Anger had Marianne wearing rather a lot of fake blood and ambling around an Arab cemetery at midnight, was puerile beyond words. She completed it, and duly flew home to her wall.

Then, when she was least expecting it, Marianne was rescued by Mike Leander, who one day found her sitting on her wall. By now, the combination of cocaine, cigarettes, and almost recurrent laryngitis had permanently affected her voice. Gone were the dulcet tones which had captivated fans with "As Tears Go By" and "Summer Nights", replaced by a harsher, gutteral sound—by no means unpleasant to listen to—which would put her into the same timbre bracket as predecessors Marianne Oswald, Damia, Dietrich, and Lotte Lenya. In time she would cover items from the repertoires of all four, and do so exceedingly well. Leander was now working for Bell Records and he coaxed her back into the studio to make a test-recording of Bob Dylan's "It's All Over Now, Baby Blue". The Bell executives were impressed, and in next to no time she had taped enough material—including songs by Joni Mitchell and James Taylor—for an entire album, *Rich Kid Blues*, hardly an appropriate title for a Marianne Faithfull release at this stage of her life which may explain why, seemingly without explanation, Bell dropped the project. It would take another fourteen years for *Rich Kid Blues* to see the light of day.

Marianne's career had suffered a setback, and so did her personal life. In March 1972, the *Reading Evening Post* reported an incident when John Dunbar tried to snatch his son, forcing the police to intervene. He subsequently applied to the courts for full custody, declaring Marianne an unfit mother— more than a little hypocritical, for he had had a drug habit, albeit not as serious as hers was now, for years. After the hearing, Nicholas went to live with Dunbar and his girlfriend, model Jean Shrimpton. Dunbar did not want Eva Faithfull looking after the boy either, in case she left him alone with Marianne. This sent Eva into a downward spiral of depression which culminated in her attempting suicide with an overdose of liquid morphine.

Aided by a new lover, Oliver Musker, Marianne began attending an NHS rehabilitation centre at Bexley Hospital. "He was like Siegfried with his blond hair, so beautiful, like a shining creature," she said of ex-Etonian Musker, two years her junior and a descendant of Mary Tudor. She recalled that he was bad tempered, which seems to have been prerequisite of most of the men she fell for. The programme helped a lot and, though by no means completely cured, she was able to work again. Director Stephen Weeks cast her as the female lead in *Ghost Story* (1974) which tells of the goings on in an old dark house—in America, it was released as *Madhouse Mansion*. Her co-stars were Larry Dann and Penelope Keith, and the locations were filmed in India, with Musker by her side. In Delhi, she met up with her old friend Robert Fraser, living in the city. She said that trekking the foothills of the Himalayas with Fraser and his mother, and the inner peace this brought, constituted one of the happiest periods of her life. The affair with Musker did not last. She also learned that her friend, Michael Cooper, had died of a heroin overdose.

Returning to London, Marianne appeared with Denholm Elliot in *Mad Dogs* at the Hampstead Theatre Club. In October 1973, David Bowie invited her to participate in his *1980 Stage Show* (a pun on George Orwell's *1984*) at the Marquee Club. The event was filmed for television, but to date has only been broadcast in America: the 200-strong invited audience of mostly over-the-top gays and transvestites was considered too much for the BBC. Marianne proved a sensation performing "As Tears Go By", and Noel Coward's "Twentieth Century Blues". Written for his 1931 West End revue, this was Brechtian in its approach—albeit tongue-in-cheek with lines such as, "In this hurly-burly of insanity, our dreams cannot last long." In his entire life, Coward had never known the meaning of hardship, while Marianne transformed it into a true *chanson du cafard*. In splendid form, she and Bowie rounded off the evening with their individual take on Sonny and Cher's "I Got You Babe"—Bowie making his final appearance as his Ziggy Stardust alter-ego, Marianne dressed as a nun, in a backless habit through which the audience saw her bare bottom as she left the stage!

Marianne was back, but there would still be some way to go before her phoenix completed its ascent from the ashes. To obliterate her past while paving the road for her future, she said, she would have to create her own Frankenstein and become the creature as well.

The *Rich Kid Blues* songs may have been assigned to a vault for now, and Bell Records may have (off the record) considered her washed up. Her former mentor Tony Calder did not think so. Now working for NEMS Records, Calder contacted Marianne during the summer of 1975 and offered her a recording contract. She maintained that this was partly out of pity, partly because of her notoriety—truthfully, she had a great deal to offer the music business. NEMS represented the songwriter Allen Reynolds, best known for his work with country singers Waylon Jennings and Crystal Gayle. Jennings' latest album was *Dreaming My Dreams*, and Marianne recorded the beautiful title-track which she sang as a gentle, lilting waltz, coupled with her own "Lady Madeleine". The lyrics of the former could easily have been about her and Mick Jagger: "Someday I'll get over you....but I'll always miss dreaming my dreams of you!" The other song was about Madeleine D'Arcy, her Irish friend who had recently died of a drugs overdose, aged twenty-seven: Marianne had found her body, and (she claimed) disposed of the evidence before the police had arrived. The record, released in November, was her best work since "Counting". She described it as "middle-European *weltschmertz*" and "a sort of country-and-western Marlene Dietrich" and she was not far wrong. It did not chart, and neither did its successor—Reynolds' "All I Wanna Do In Life"—but it gave a clear indication that Marianne Faithfull the singer, as opposed to Marianne Faithfull the "scandalous personality" was back. It *did* rocket to the top of the Irish charts, where it remained for seven weeks inspiring the record company to follow up the single with the "reposing" album. Marianne had triumphed with pop and folk, and was now hoping to do so with a Gram Parsons-style "country roots album with Celtic vibes"—also titled *Dreaming My Dreams*. This would be released in January 1977, withdrawn a year later, and replaced with *Faithless* with four extra tracks. It contained several classics including Bob Johnson's "Wait For Me Down By The River", Bob Dylan's "I'll Be Your Baby Tonight", and J D Miller's "Honky Tonk Angels", recorded as a tribute to Parsons, who had died of an accidental overdose in October 1973.

The next man in Marianne's life was Ben Brierly, the bassist with the punk outfit the Vibrators, a former heroin addict she met whilst buying smack from the house in Fulham Road where he was staying. At 24, he was five years her junior. "He was just recovering from hepatitis and he looked pale and interesting in that leather, drug-addicted way," she recalled, "And I fell in love with him."

Marianne maintained that the one with Salford-born Brierly was the most passionate relationship of her life, but the one which caused her the most pain because of his serial adultery. She, who admitted to playing the field in the past, was turning into a one-man woman. Brierly asked her to move into his flat—actually on loan from a friend, who turfed them out soon afterwards, resulting in them living in a squat without electricity or water. NEMS were paying Marianne £100 a week as part of her contract, but most of this went on drugs. She and Brierly toured briefly as part of her NEMS deal, though not with great success—he was, she said, a good songwriter but useless as a bassist. Also as she had latterly walked in Mick Jagger's shadow, so Brierly would walk in hers—a great source of dissention between them.

Marianne had taken a risk with *Come My Way*, and it had worked. *Dreaming My Dreams*/*Faithless* proved less commercial, but she was moving in the right direction and things would get better. As she returned to live performances, she initially preferred Ireland because Ireland had provided her with her only chart-topper, and because the Irish press were less judgmental than their English counterparts.

She soon realised that it would not be possible to sustain her career in such limited circumstances, and in the autumn of 1978 she made her London comeback with concerts at The Music Machine, and Dingwalls—non-intrusive venues where audiences would not expect too much should things go wrong. Those who had not seen her for a while were surprised to hear her singing "As Tears Go By", not just slower than on the 1964 recording but an octave lower. If anything, "Dreaming My Dreams" was too classy a number for such rowdy establishments, though several other songs from the *Faithless* album, especially "Honky Tonk Angels" and Allen Reynolds' "Wrong Road Again" went down inordinately well. *Melody Maker*'s Ian Birch liked what he heard, if some of his colleagues pretended not to, and hailed her "this elegantly ravaged outsider".

On 8 June 1979, Marianne and Ben Brierly were married at the Chelsea Registry Office. A special guest was the Sex Pistol's Johnny Rotten. Not so long before, Marianne had been approached by sexploitation movie director Russ Meyer to play Ma

99

Vicious (Sid's mother) in his biopic of the Sex Pistols. Initially, she had accepted—then, aware of the effect the role might have on her already shady reputation in some quarters, she had backed down and Meyer had shelved the film. Interviewed by the press, Marianne "did a Liz Taylor", mirroring Taylor's stock statements to the press after each of her marriages, telling reporters, "Ben and I are very happy together. I expect to spend the rest of my life with him."

One of the songs performed at The Music Machine was Heathcote Williams' copiously vulgar, "Why D'Ya Do It?"—a rant against infidelity, the likes of which few had heard since the under-counter filth-for-filth's-sake outpourings of the Peter Cook-Dudley Moore alter-egos, Derek and Clive. Williams was a Cheshire-born poet, playwright, actor, and generally despicable individual who had famously been sent down from Oxford after turning up to sit his finals, wearing as SS officer's uniform. "Why D'Ya Do It?" contains so many profanities that it is virtually impossible to quote a single line without coming across at least one. Initially, he had wanted to give the song to Tina Turner, who one imagines would never have sung it in a million years! Marianne's response to Turner doing her song, set to a near-tuneless riff from Jimi Hendrix's "All Along The Watchtower", was, "The day *she* does it, I'll give up." Producer Mark Miller Mundy was enthralled by it, and Eva Faithfull regarded it as a work of art. Mundy went out of his way to introduce her to Chris Blackwell of Island Records, who agreed that the piece would complement the current punk wave. Forty years earlier, Lotte Lenya had shocked audiences with her portrayal of the dockside whore in Brecht and Weill's *The Threepenny Opera*, her Pirate Jenny poring scorn on the harbour low-life from her brothel window—but nothing remotely like this piece which nevertheless so impressed Mundy that he was willing to inject his own cash into ensuring that Marianne recorded it for posterity. Yet had she *not* recorded it, her comeback might never have happened.

Marianne assembled a fine band of musicians, headed by guitarist Barry Reynolds and Steve Winwood, formerly of the Spencer Davis Group, on synthesiser. She recorded "Why D'Ya Do It?" at the Matrix Studios, reputedly putting so much into her performance that she collapsed from exhaustion. For the B-side she chose her own "Broken English", co-written with Reynolds and inspired by the German terrorist Ulrike Meinhof (1934-76) of the infamous Bader-Meinhof gang. Charged with murder and other atrocities, she had hanged herself in her cell halfway through her trial. Film of her interrogation had referred to her speaking in "broken English", hence the connection. Island planned releasing the songs on a single even though warned that few radio stations would be allowed to play them. There were problems when workers at EMI, subcontracted by Island for packing and distribution, staged a walk-out after hearing the tracks at a union meeting. Chris Blackwell however knew when he was on to a good thing and gave the go-ahead for Marianne to record an album, using *Broken English* as its title. It would be brief affair— eight songs running to just 38 minutes, and owing to a combination of health problems and perfectionism would take six months to finish but prove worthy of a place in any fan's connection if only for her stunning interpretations of John Lennon's "Working Class Hero", "The Ballad Of Lucy Jordan", and her own "Guilt", inspired by her Catholic upbringing.

"The Ballad Of Lucy Jordan" was from the pen of Shel Silverstein, who had written "A Boy Named Sue" for Johnny Cash. Dr Hook recorded it first, but thanks to Marianne's definitive reading, few remember this version now. It *belongs* to her, and has been used on the soundtrack of several films, notably *Thelma And Louise* (1991). Marianne sang it, in her role as God, in a hilarious episode of French & Saunders' comedy series, *Absolutely Fabulous*, with Anita Pallenberg playing the Devil! Superbly accompanied by Steve Winwood, this iconic *chanson-réaliste* tells the story of the lonely, frustrated housewife who has nothing to do all day but rearrange the flowers and dream of riding through the streets of Paris in an open-top sports car with the wind blowing through her hair. The kind of life, Marianne said, she would have been forced to endure had she married Gene Pitney and found herself holed up in a Connecticut mansion. Lucy almost gets her wish when she climbs up onto the roof of her apartment block—but the man who reaches out to take her hand is a paramedic, and the "long white car" she rides in is an ambulance, sent to escort her to a mental hospital. Great stuff!

Three songs from *Broken English*—the title-track, "Witches Song", and "Lucy Jordan"—formed a 13-minute video shot by controversial director Derek Jarman, whose punk film, *Jubilee*, Marianne very admired. One has to say however that parts of it are not too complimentary. The production looks cheap, much of it comprising several films projected on top of each other at the same time. The images in the "Lucy Jordan" segment, where a very glamorous Marianne walks through Soho and Piccadilly late at night in a short skirt, also make her look like *une fille du trottoir*. Marianne and Jarman, who died of an AIDS-related illness in 1994, became friends: in 1987 she sang "The Skye Boat Song" in his anti-Margaret Thatcher film, *The Last Of England.*

Marianne's private life however was not quite so successful. In the past she had never minded lovers cheating on her—much of the time, playing them at their own game had been part of the fun. Now, she wanted to settle down, but she was too involved with her work to realise that Ben Brierly was having affairs with women both at home and in Los Angeles, where he had been working on one of his own projects while she had been recording *Broken English*. When he returned to London, the writing was clearly on the wall. "Why D'Ya Do It?", she later said, had been all about her anger towards him.

Because she had taken such a daring, no-holds-barred controversial stance, Marianne had put herself at a distinct advantage over her Brit Girl colleagues. While musically they stood still once the Sixties were over, or reverted to frequently bland, middle-of-the-road ditties, or used iconic pop stars as crutches to establish brief comebacks, Marianne strode out alone and grabbed the music scene by the balls. Whilst they faded, she only flourished.

With Ben Brierly on their wedding day.

With Jennifer Saunders.

7: Phoenix Rising

The Jagger connection would always be there, but the further Marianne progressed, the less it would occupy centre-stage. Even the *Sun*, the first British tabloid to have mocked her downfall, could not help praising *Broken English*. The frequently acerbic columnist Nina Myskow wrote a feature headed, "Jagger's Bird Bounces Back", and observed, "After the Swinging Sixties, let's hope she makes it to the top again in the Exciting Eighties." The *New Musical Express*, entering its cynical phase which would only get worse to the extent that some reviews had little or nothing to do with the item or person being reviewed, opined of the album's raw, partially-autobiographical content, "She has pasted sequins on her scars and charged admission for customers to come and gawk at them." In America, *Rolling Stone* called it, "A stunning account of the life that goes on after the end—an awful, liberating, harridan's laugh at the life that came before."

Broken English was the resurrection of Marianne Faithfull. She still had a way to go regarding her drug problem, but now had a solid base from which to fight her way back to the top. The album was not a huge commercial success in Britain despite the critical acclaim, but it went gold across Europe— platinum in Germany, on account of the Bader-Meinhof connection. She was invited to sing in New York and as the result of a few high jinks with Anita Pallenberg, messed up an appearance on *Saturday Night Live*—claiming she had over-exerted herself during rehearsals. She followed the album with *Dangerous Acquaintances*—more mainstream rock than its predecessor, less crude, and aside from two songs—Marianne's "Sweetheart" and "Ben Brierly's "Intrigue"—less exciting and regarded by many fans as a let-down. The Americans liked it, and this—along with her constantly being harassed by the British police who she said assumed that anyone making a record like *Broken English* could *only* be a drug-dealer—saw her relocating to New York. There were other reasons for her now wishing to leave Britain. She recalled watching footage of the Falklands War on the television, and of the Pope "playing" Wembley: "I just thought, I've got to get out of here. I can't bear to stay in this country a minute longer." Additionally, she was having problems with her marriage, and maybe thought that a change of scenery might stop it from floundering completely. She and Brierly rented an apartment on New York's East 18th Street and initially survived, she said, on coke and smack.

Marianne's next album, the mostly self-composed *A Child's Adventure*, was recorded at the very zenith of her addiction, not that one can tell while listening to it. The highlights were Ben Brierly's "Falling From Grace" with him on backing vocals, and Barry Reynolds' desolately brilliant "Times Square", reminiscent of Edith Piaf's "La ville inconnue"—the unknown town where, the more one sees, the less one needs to belong. Then one day Marianne came home and walked in on Brierly and his mistress. Inasmuch as *she* had searched for an excuse to leave Mick Jagger, so Brierly wanted to opt out. "Ben told me later that he'd hoped I would die, because it would make things easier," she said, earning him few favours with her fans. In the wake of this latest drama, Marianne left New York and spent several months in Jamaica. Whilst here she learned that Brierly had been arrested and charged with being involved with a heroin-dealing gang, and deported.

In 1985, Marianne added another string to her bow when she recorded "Ballad Of The Soldier's Wife", featured on Hal Willner's *Lost In The Stars: The Music of Kurt Weill*—the others highlights included Lou Reed's "September Song", and Dagmar Krause's "Surabaya Johnny". Marianne's voice, deep and raspy, was perfectly suited to the anarchic works of Brecht and Weill, who wrote the song as a response to the Battle of Stalingrad, after being exiled to America. One cannot be trained to adequately perform Brecht and Weill—the ability to do so must be innate, and in Marianne's case her sensibility in dipping into so eclectic a catalogue may have been inherited from her mother, who had lived the Weimar experience which had ended in 1933 with Hitler's rise to power. Weill's wife, Lotte Lenya, had introduced much of their work on the stage during these years, and had seen her own voice change dramatically the way Marianne's had. In the Thirties, Lenya had been possessed of a sweet, almost innocent tone. By 1955, when she recorded her *Berlin Theatre Songs* album, chain-smoking had brought about the gravelly tone for which she is revered. "One octave below laryngitis" was how one critic described it. There are many who regard Marianne as the finest British interpreter of Brecht and Weill. "Ballad Of The Soldier's Wife" is by far and above her best song interpretation of the 1990s, and easily compares with the definitive 1969 version by French *chanteuse* Pia Colombo.

Marianne's renewed success did little to curb the moments of hopelessness as she battled to overcome her drug problem. In November 1985, while living with a man she never named but denounced as "a desperate, desperate junkie....just another form of Ben, a comrade in getting high," there was an incident which may have been a second suicide attempt, but more than likely a self-induced wake-up call. Marianne shot up on as much smack as she could find in the room, fell, and broke her jaw. This, she claimed, led to an out-of-body experience: she was actually dead, in a strange place and amongst strangers, but able to ask herself, "Is this how you want to end your life?" Clearly, she did not: she survived the experience and, with the help of Island's Chris Blackwell, entered the Hazelden Clinic in Minneapolis. Off and on, as her jaw refused to heal properly and became severely infected, she stayed here for six months. Part of her treatment after the first month involved counselling others, and she formed an attachment to a former deejay, Howard Tose, an addict who additionally suffered from bi-polar disorder and Tourette's. Following her discharge from the clinic, with a clean bill of health, she moved with Tose to his home city of Boston where they rented an apartment in the Harbor Towers Building. It was here in March 1986 that she learned of her friend Robert Fraser's death from an AIDS-related illness. Aged 48, he was one of the first British celebrities to succumb to the disease. Only weeks later, during what appears to have been a psychotic episode, Howard Tose flung himself to his death from the 36th Floor window. Marianne left the block as soon as the paramedics had removed his body: she rented a house in Cambridge, Massachusetts, and as had happened in Australia, her mother flew out to be with her.

Marianne's rock-blues-show tunes album, *Strange Weather*, produced by Hal Willner, was dedicated to Howard Tose's memory, and released at around the time she and Ben Brierly were divorced. This was a dramatic, often mournful anthology which is at the same time pleasantly and surprisingly uplifting. The title-track was by Tom Waits, and deals with the very English trait of always discussing the weather. It is ingenious in that it sounds like it could just as easily been written in Thirties, and as such would crop up regularly in concerts, slotted between the Brecht and Weill numbers. Equally interesting are Marianne's takes on the classics: Al Dubin and Harry Warren's "Boulevard Of Broken Dreams", from their 1934 film, *Moulin Rouge*, is a gem—as is Jerome Kern's "Yesterdays". She re-recorded "As Tears Go" for this album and, almost a quarter-century on, the lyrics were more suited to her than they had been back in 1964. "Forty is the age to sing it, not seventeen," she told *Vogue*. A veritable tragedy was someone at Island's decision *not* to include Marianne's version of "Gloomy Sunday"— fans would have to wait a little longer for this amazing piece which had emerged from Hungary in the early Thirties, as "The Budapest Suicide Song". The most famous recording was by the Damia, "Sombre dimanche", banned in Britain and America because of its subject matter. In the Damia version, the woman's lover has left her and she chooses a romantic death—she will enter their room, her arms filled with flowers, and end it all. He will find her with her eyes wide open, but friends will beg him not to cry because she has died to prove how much she loved him! Billie Holiday had performed the song in English, but even she had not sung it as well as Marianne.

In 1988, Marianne married for a third time. Giorgio Della Terza was an Italian-born actor and writer, who she met in Massachusetts at a Narcotics Anonymous meeting. The marriage would last until 1991. Soon afterwards she met Francois Ravard, an enigmatic Frenchman who became her manager, and who would be there for the long haul. "He helps me channel my energy in a positive way," she told the *Independent On Sunday* in October 2004, "When I look at what I can really do when I'm firing on all cylinders, I think it's a shame that I didn't start cracking along more quickly."

On 21 July, Marianne flew to Berlin to appear in *The Wall,* former Pink Floyd's Roger Waters' all-star extravaganza staged to commemorate the collapse of the Berlin Wall. The event was filmed and broadcast around the world. Marianne appeared in a scene entitled "The Trial", alongside Ute Lemper and Albert Finney. "A load of old rubbish," observed Marlene Dietrich, with whom I had part-scripted a speech when the wall had come down. That same year she triumphed with her album, *Blazing Away*, a retrospective of her life and career recorded at St Anne's Cathedral, Brooklyn the previous November. Marianne returned here, seven years later, to appear in a tribute to drowned singer Jeff Buckley. The opener was Edith Piaf's "Les prisons du roi"—the simple story of the man locked up for stealing a jewel for his sweetheart, and who begs the King to lock her up with him, for she too is a thief, having stolen his heart. Towards the end of the performance, she sang "She Moved Thru The Fair" as a truly inspirational dirge-like chant.

In May 1992, Eva Faithfull died of cancer, aged eighty. During her youth and early on in her career, Marianne had fought to get away from this woman, who nevertheless had always been there to help her through her traumas. The greatest of these had been the one in Australia, and it was ironic that Marianne should have been touring this country at the time. She flew home at once. As had happened on the eve of her marriage to John Dunbar, she picked wild flowers—primarily hawthorn blossom—with which she decorated Eva's coffin.

Shortly after losing her mother, Marianne, who had recently relocated to County Kildare, sang the role of Jenny Towler in Frank McGuiness's new translation of Brecht and Weill's *The Threepenny Opera* at Dublin's Gate Theatre. For two months, each performance sold out. In 1993, she became a grandmother when Nicholas and his actress wife, Carole Jahme, had a boy which they baptised Oscar, after Oscar Wilde. This year too, she completed her memoirs. Her story, she said, needed to be told. She denounced a biography by Mark Hodkinson in which she failed to recognise herself as "scaly", adding, "He was counting on my keeling over at any moment. He has said in the British press that any day now he expects to hear that I've overdosed in some street corner lavatory. Dream on!" Few show business autobiographies have been as poignant and uncompromisingly honest as *Faithfull*.

111

In 1995, Marianne teamed up with Brooklyn-born Italianate musician-producer Angelo Badalamenti, who had recently composed the soundtracks for *Blue Velvet* and the *Twin Peaks* television series. The result was *A Secret Life*, a lushly orchestrated concept album containing just eight songs, with a prologue by Dante, and an epilogue by Shakespeare. The best tracks were "Bored By Dreams", partially sung in French—and "She", neither the Charles Aznavour nor the Gram Parsons song, but an original composition by herself, set to a haunting refrain poignantly evoking the bygone age of the irreplaceable Hollywood movie.

The following year, having tested the waters with Hal Willner's Kurt Weill tribute album and *The Threepenny Opera*, Marianne put on her Weimar hat once more and recorded *20th Century Blues*, quite possibly her best album since *Love In A Mist*. Her first for RCA Victor, this too was produced by Willner, and is as articulate as it is spellbinding: fifteen songs so well-orchestrated and performed that picking a favourite is impossible. Marianne had already performed Weill's *Seven Deadly Sins* at St Anne's Church, Brooklyn, and since put together her showcase, *An Evening At The Weimar Republic*. This she had taken around the world, and the album comprised a live performance in Paris at Le Morning Club. Brecht and Weill were represented by "The Alabama Song", "Pirate Jenny", and Frank McGuinness's new English adaptation of "Mack The Knife". There was a stunning reading of "La complainte de la Seine", originally performed by Lys Gauty, and ending with a bar from Piaf's "Mon légionnaire". There were songs by Brecht and Weill contemporaries: Noel Coward's "Twentieth Century Blues", and Friedrich Hollander's "Falling In Love Again" and "Illusions", both introduced by Marlene Dietrich—who died two weeks after Eva Faithfull. Marianne finally got around to recording *The Seven Deadly Sins* with the Vienna Radio Orchestra in 1998. The *New York Times*' John Rockwell, an avid Lotte Lenya fan, declared her the best interpreter of Weill since Lenya, and enthused, "She handled her part with a fine blend of dramatic world-weariness, quivering timbral allure, conviction of phrasing and bitterness of declaration." Marianne had proved, ultimately, that with this kind of material she had found her niche. Who would have thought that a shy convent schoolgirl from Reading would one day be compared with the greatest of the European *sprechsingers*? "It's probably because I was listening to Lotte Lenya in my mother's womb," she mused. Vienna also brought sadness, for whilst she was here recording the album she received news from Brazier's that her father had died, aged 85. Marianne asked the trumpeter from the Radio Orchestra to play the "Last Post"—she recorded this, and a few days later had it played at Glynn Faithfull's funeral.

Marianne's output was not just restricted to singing and acting. A few days before the Christmas of 2000, while relaxing at her new Dublin home she received a call from her friend Gregory Corso. The beat-poet was dying of cancer, and needed her and Hal Willner to fly out to Minnesota to co-produce what would be a posthumous album of his work. Her response was that he should not "croak" until they arrived in January. She spent several days with

113

Corso, and read three poems for the album, entitled *Die On Me*. One week later, Corso died, aged 70.

Despite numerous set-backs due to poor health, Marianne's recording and film career has not diminished in the 2000s. In 2001 she appeared with Lambert Wilson in *Far From China*. Five years later she portrayed Empress Marie-Thérése in Sofia Coppola's *Marie Antoinette*. In *Irina Palm*, she played a 60-year-old widow who becomes a sex worker to pay for medical treatment for her seriously ill grandson. Her performance was nominated for a European Film Award at the Berlin Film Festival—she lost out to Helen Mirren.

Vagabond Ways, released in 2000, was Marianne's first album of original material since *A Secret Life*, and was produced by Canadian singer-songwriter Daniel Lanois. Gram Parson's last singing partner, Emmylou Harris, provided some of the backing vocals. Included were songs by Leonard Cohen and Elton John, but the *piéce de résistance* was the gorgeous title-track, penned by Marianne and David Courts, who among other things fashioned skull rings for Keith Richards! "I drink and I take drugs....I had my first baby at fourteen," the girl tells the doctor before having an enforced hysterectomy. In true *chanteuse-réaliste* fashion, Marianne puts herself into the girl's shoes.

Kissin' Time (2002), contained songs penned by such contemporary musicians as Jarvis Cocker and French *enfant terrible* Étienne Daho. The highlight was Marianne's collaboration with Dave Stewart, "Song For Nico", her stunning tribute to the Velvet Underground singer. Nico (Christa Paffgen, 1938-88) had begun her career in 1958—as a walk-on in a

Mario Lanza film—and spent the next thirty years developing her icon status while in a permanently drugged haze. There had been a much-publicised affair with Brian Jones—"When Brian is near, Nico doesn't feel so queer," Marianne pronounces—and a fling with Alain Delon which had resulted in Nico having his son. Delon had always denied paternity, even though his parents had raised the boy. In the song, Marianne pays "homage" to her *Girl On A Motorcycle* co-star by calling him a "cunt".

Three years later, Marianne released *Before The Poison*, which saw her working with Nick Cave, Blur's Damon Albarn, and P J Harvey. That same year she recorded a tribute to Serge Gainsbourg: "Lola Rastaquoere" was one of the tracks on the *Monsieur Gainsbourg Revisted* album, a dreadful compilation of which the least said the better. In 2008 she released the highly acclaimed *Easy Come, Easy Go*, a double-album (title courtesy of the Bessie Smith classic) produced by Hal Willner which included duets with Rufus Wainwright, Sean Lennon, Jarvis Cocker, and her old friend Keith Richards with whom she paid tribute to Gram Parsons with an intensely moving "Sing Me Back Home". Other highlights included Randy Newman's "In Germany Before The War", a fantastic late-night reading of Peggy Lee's "Black Coffee", Dolly Parton's "Down From Dover", Judy Sill's "The Phoenix", and Morrissey's "Dear God Please Help Me". Its only negative track is "Somewhere", from *West Side Story*—essential listening if only to hear what seems to be Marianne impersonating Tallulah Bankhead's infamous tuneless drawl, and to hear how unbelievably *bad* Jarvis Cocker sounds. Really, this one might have been better left *off* the album—it's saving grace being that it runs into the excellent folk song, "Flandyke Shore", which Marianne sings with Rufus Wainwright's mother and aunt, Kate and Anne McGarrigle.

At the end of 2004, Marianne was forced to cancel part of a world tour owing to exhaustion. Two years later, another was shelved when she was diagnosed with breast cancer. Thankfully, her doctors caught this in time, operated on her, and a few months later she was given a clean bill of health. "To me, there is nothing like being on stage," she told a *Daily Telegraph* reporter in the spring of 2009, "It kills all the aches and pains!"

In January 2011, Marianne released her eighteenth studio album, *Horses & High Heels*, a collection of thirteen songs, four of which were co-written by her. Many believed the finest songs on the album were her versions of Dusty Springfield's "Goin' Back" and the Shangri Las' "Past, Present, Future". The album received mixed reviews in Britain, but was much-acclaimed on the Continent when Marianne embarked on an extensive tour of Europe. On 23 March, that year, she was awarded the *Commandeur of the Ordre des Arts et des Lettres*, one of France's most prestigious cultural honours.

Three years later, *Give My Love To London* was released to huge international acclaim, and her last album to date (2016) is *No Exit* released with a companion DVD which sees her reviving one of her finest earlier songs, "Come And Stay With Me."

And when the time comes, she had been asked by *Clash* magazine in 2009...would she like to bow out gracefully or release one last amazing album and go out with a bang?

"I'd like to go out with a bang, yeah," she responded.

Let us hope that there will be *many* amazing albums before this time comes. Maybe it is a worn cliché, but when they made Marianne Faithfull, they broke the mold.

Marianne in Paris, autumn 2016.

Marianne Faithfull: 1960s Vinyl Discography

1964

As Tears Go By/ Greensleeves (Decca F11923)

Blowin' In The Wind (Decca, unreleased take, 24 September)

Blowing In The Wind/ House Of The Rising Sun (1) (Decca F12007)

Greensleeves; As Tears Go By; Blowin' In The Wind; House Of The Rising Sun (extended single) Decca 457.049 France only

1965

Come And Stay With Me/ What Have I Done Wrong (Decca F12075)

This Little Bird/ Morning Sun (Decca F12162)

Go Away From My World; Go Away From My World; The Most Of What Is Least; Et maintenant; The Sha La La Song (EP) Decca FE 8624

This Little Bird; Morning Sun; Come And Stay With Me; What Have I Done Wrong (extended single) Decca 457.068 France only

Marianne Faithfull: Come And Stay With Me; If I Never Get To Love You; Time Takes Time; He'll Come Back To Me; Down Town; Plaisir d'amour; Can't You Hear My Heartbeat; As Tears Go By; Paris Bells; They Will Never Leave You; What Have They Done To The Rain; In My Time Of Sorrow; What Have I Done Wrong; I'm A Loser (Album) Decca LK4689 UK release

(Album) London LL3423/PS423 US release. As above, minus Down Town; Can't You Hear My Heartbeat

(Album) London LL3423/PS423 US re-release, same catalogue number as above, but with This Little Bird replacing They Will Never Leave You

Come My Way: Come My Way (1); Jabberwock; Portland Town; House Of The Rising Sun (2); Spanish Is A Loving Tongue; Fare Thee Well; Lonesome Traveller; Down In The Salley Garden; Mary Ann (1); Full Fathom Five; Four Strong Winds; Black Girl; Once I Had A Sweetheart; Bells Of Freedom (Album) Decca LK4688

119

Un piccolo cuore (This Little Bird); Quando ballai con lui (Morning Sun) Derby DB 5141 Italy only

Summer Nights; Sha La La Song (Decca F12193)

Summer Nights; The Sha La La Song; Go Away From My World; The Most Of What Is Least (extended single) Decca 457.085 France only

Summer Nights; Go Away From My World (Decca 72040) France only

Yesterday; Oh, Look Around You (Decca F12268)

Yesterday; Oh, Look Around You; Can't You Hear My Heartbeat; Paris Bells (EP) Decca 457.097 released *before* 457.094 (see below)

Go Away From My World: Go Away From My World; Yesterday; Come My Way (1); The Last Thing On My Mind; How Should I Your True Love Know; Wild Mountain Thyme; Summer Nights; Mary Ann (2); Scarborough Fair; Lullaby; North Country Maid; Sally Free And Easy. (album) London LL3452 US release

1966
A bientot nous deux (He'll Come Back To Me); Nuits d'été (Summer Nights); La...devant toi (Come And Stay With Me); Comme une aube nouvelle (Morning Sun) (EP) Decca 457.094 France only

A bientot nous deux; La...devant toi (Decca 72.058) France only

North Country Maid: Green Are Your Eyes; Scarborough Fair; Cockleshells; The Last Thing On My Mind; The First Time Ever I Saw Your Face; Sally Free And Easy; Sunny Goodge Street; How Should I Your True Love Know; She Moved Thru The Fair; North Country Maid; Lullaby; Wild Mountain Thyme (album) Decca LK4778

Tomorrow's Calling; That's Right Baby (Decca F12408)

Coquillages; Si demain (Tomorrow's Calling); Le coeur gros; Ne me quitte pas (Les Parapluies de Cherbourg) (EP) Decca 457.119 France only

Counting; I'd Like To Dial Your Number (Decca F12443)

Hang Onto A Dream/ Rosie, Rosie (Decca, unreleased) Released 1988 on the CD version of *Love In A Mist*.

Counting; I'd Like To Dial Your Number; Sunny Goodge Street; That's Right Baby (EP) Decca 457.125 France only

Faithfull Forever: Counting; Tomorrow's Calling; The First Time; With You In Mind; In The Night Time; Ne me quitte pas; Monday Monday; Some Other Spring; That's Right Baby; Lucky Girl; I'm The Sky; I Have A Love (album) London LL3482 US release

1967
Hier ou demain; North Country Maid; Green Are Your Eyes; Sally Free And Easy (EP) Decca 457.139 France only

Ce chi spera; Oh, Look Around You (Derby DB 5171) Italy only

Painting Box (Decca, unreleased duet with Paul McCartney, accompanied by Jon Mark) 3 February

Love In A Mist: Yesterday; You Can't Go Where The Roses Go; Our Love Has Gone; Don't Make Promises; In The Night Time; This Little Bird; Ne me quitte pas; Counting; Reason To Believe; Coquillages; With You In Mind; Young Girl Blues; Good Guy; I Have A Love (album) Decca LK4852

With A Little Help From My Friends/ English Summer (Decca, unreleased) The former by Lennon & McCartney, the latter by Jagger & Richards

Is This What I Get For Loving You; Tomorrow's Calling (Decca F12524)

1969
Something Better; Sister Morphine (Decca F12899)

122

The World Of Marianne Faithfull: As Tears Go By; This Little Bird; Summer Nights; Scarborough Fair; Monday Monday; Come And Stay With Me; Is This What I Get For Loving You; Yesterday; Tomorrow's Calling; In My Time Of Sorrow; Go Away From My World (album) Decca PA17 Released in the USA as *Marianne Faithfull's Greatest Hits* (London PS547)

2008 (recorded 1965-6)
Marianne Faithfull: Live At The BBC. 13th May 1965: Can't You Hear My Heartbeat; Come And Stay With Me; In My Time Of Sorrow. 5th June 1965: Go Away From My World; The Sha La La Song; This Little Bird. 24th July 1965: Go Away From My World; Paris Bells; Summer Nights. 18th December 1965: Lullaby; The Last Thing On My Mind; Yesterday. 31st May 1966: As Tears Go By; Cockleshells; Tomorrow's Calling. Marianne's appearances on BBC Radio's *The Saturday Club*, interspersed with short interviews. Presented by Brian Matthews. (CD album) Decca 5307959

Sandie Shaw

Known as the Barefoot Princess from Dagenham, she was one of the decade's most alluring images. The typical girl-next-door, with no airs and graces, she was plucked from a talent show and discovered by pop sensation Adam Faith, whose fame she soon superceded with the help of a shared, shrewd martinet manager. She topped the UK charts three times, had scores of hits in four languages across the Continent and won the Eurovision Song Contest at a time when the songs were worth listening to. Then, while at the peak of her career, she stepped away from the music scene to raise a family and embrace Buddhism—only to make a spectacular return a few years later, fronting the Smiths. Yet despite her fame, talent and immense popularity, then as in her Sixties heyday Sandie was always looking for excuses *not* to perform—and finally she bowed out to devote her life to her new vocation, that of show business psychoanalyst.

1: Had A Dream Last Night

She was born Sandra Ann Goodrich in Dagenham, Essex, on 26 February 1947. Wanting to become a singer, as a child she attended churches of differing denominations *just* to participate in the singing, and was one of only three students in her year to pass her eleven-plus. She left school with qualifications for a place at the Robert Clack Technical College, yet eschewed this to work as a punch-card operator at the town's British Motors plant. Reasonably well-paid, she was the first to admit she never exerted herself: "I spent most of my working hours in the sick bay with real or simulated period cramps."

Tall (5 feet 8 inches in her stocking feet), gangly, awkward, myopic and plain (or so she considered herself), she appears to have been the proverbial wallflower when weekend socialising. To this end, towards the end of 1963 she entered a talent contest at the Ilford Palais—where Kathy Kirby's career had begun—in the hope of getting boys to dance with her. What she sang is not known, only that she came second and that this led to her being contacted by music publisher Terry Oates, who invited her to travel to London for an audition. Supervised by Oates and Jimmy Henny, a deejay with Radio Luxembourg, she sang two songs—one was Doris Day's 1958 hit, "Everybody Loves A Lover"—accompanied by Tony Rivers & The Castaways, a local band managed by Oates. Impressed, Oates took her under his wing—though she would not stay here for long—engaging Sandra and The Castaways for a charity show, organised by Henny, at the Hammersmith Commodore. Sponsored by Silvikrin shampoo, this was broadcast live by Radio Luxembourg in April 1964. Also on the bill were The Hollies and The Swinging Blue Jeans: the headliners were Adam Faith & The Roulettes.

Wearing a white catalogue dress and pink sling-backs, Sandra should have performed three songs, but nerves got the better of her—her entire family and dozens of friends were sitting in the audience—and she rushed off stage after her second number. Adam Faith did not actually hear her sing, but after hearing The Roulette's guitarist, Russ Ballard, enthusing how good she was, he invited her to his dressing room for a private audition. Maybe Sandra should have read more into this, but such was her naivety that, accompanied by Ballard, she reprised "Everybody Loves A Lover" for the pint-sized, hiccupping singer. Faith was "bowled over" by her perfectly toned voice, though she was not initially impressed by him.

"I was shocked rigid," she said, "He was so tiny that even in his Cuban heels and platform soles he barely scraped my shoulder. But he was charming—the gentleman, even, in his Cockney way."

Adam Faith, though still a big hit with fans, had seen his commercial career sliding of late. In 1965 he graced the Top Twenty with a cover of Marlene Dietrich's "Message To Martha"—itself purloined from Dionne Warwick—but soon afterwards fell by the wayside until achieving considerable success with his acting career. Faith is generally acknowledged with discovering Sandie Shaw, as she became, though with an ulterior motive. She would find out some years later that he had been pocketing a sizeable percentage of her earnings.

"Dear Adam," she recalled, "He may never have been a great singer, but he was always a fine businessman."

It was Faith who that same evening introduced Sandra to his manager, Eve Taylor—a fearsome martinet who would get along with her much better than she did with Faith and her other acts. In her mid-forties, she was aptly described as resembling Ruth Ellis, the last British woman to hang. Something of a siren in her younger days, Taylor had worked the variety circuit—doing nothing special, just a sexy little fan-dance with a lot of Marilyn Monroe-style pouting. When she entered Sandie's life she looked like a cross between the caricature of a 1940s B-movies burlesque queen and feisty television cook Fannie Cradock: far too much pancake make-up, pencilled eyebrows, and her hair swept so far back that she looked like she was going bald. She chain-smoked, and could out-curse a sailor on shore leave Always on the lookout for fresh new talent Taylor did not initially share Faith's enthusiasm for the budding songstress—she is alleged to have denounced her as "crap"—and elected to give her a miss, only to change her mind a few days later after being nagged relentlessly by her "golden boy", who had promised Sandra, "Don't worry, luv. I'll fix it for ya. You're gonna be a star!"

It was Eve Taylor's "Jewish as matzo balls" husband, Moishe, who awarded the new protegée her new name—first coming up with Sandie More, then after seeing her bare size seven-and-a-half feet, Sandie Shore, which he pronounced "Shaw". Taylor, however, was not satisfied just with changing her name. Within days of taking Sandie on

127

she effected a complete transformation: ordering clothes from the best West End boutiques, sending her to Vidal Sassoon for a new hairstyle, then to a beauty salon for a complete makeover. Gone were the catalogue dresses, cheap jewellery, and the heavily lacquered hair which Sandie said resembled well-licked candyfloss. In her place was a tall, very elegant and very beautiful young woman—the only other Brit Girls who compared with her, looks-wise, would be Marianne and Kathy Kirby. The gimmick came a little later, when Sandie was working in the studio and kicked off her shoes to feel more comfortable. Taylor claimed that she sang better without them, and they would stay off for the rest of her career. Not wearing shoes also drew attention from Sandie's somewhat awkward stance when she was on the stage or in front of the television cameras—without them she tended to stoop less.

Eve Taylor sent Sandie to Tony Hatch, then a staff producer with Pye who had enjoyed great success with his girlfriend (later his wife) Jackie Trent, The Searchers, and most especially Petula Clark, who would soon record his "Downtown". Hatch got her into the studio very quickly and, under the watchful eye of Adam Faith she recorded two demos. She wanted to cover something by The Crystals or The Shirelles, but Hatch coaxed her into cutting up-tempo versions of Doris Day's "Secret Love" and Susan Maughan's "Bobby's Girl"—neither of which she could stand. These were hawked around the record companies. Decca, Parlophone, and even Pye themselves were amongst the major labels who rejected her, though the latter had a change of heart when Eve Taylor declared that Sandie's debut single should be an independent production, unheard of in those days, financed by herself and leased to the record company. This way, Taylor and "silent partner" Adam Faith—and not the record company executives—would be able to choose her material. The downside was that though she was offered a contract—countersigned by her parents because she was only seventeen—there would be no advance on sales. Taylor dismissed anything that Hatch had to offer, and brought in 22-year-old Romford-born singer-songwriter Chris Andrews, who lived around the corner from Sandie in Dagenham.

Andrews' name would become synonymous with that of Sandie Shaw. Like Burt Bacharach, though not as renowned internationally, Andrews was a master of tricky chord and key-change, and with Sandie and her pleasantly curious voice had found the perfect muse for his work. He began his career at the 2i's Coffee Bar, in Soho, and his television debut was on *Oh, Boy!* in 1959. In 1963 his "The First Time" revived Adam Faith's flagging career and gave him a Number 5 hit: others had followed. Andrews' "As Long As You're Happy, Baby", which producer-songwriter Charles Blackwell had earmarked for Samantha Jones, was now given to Sandie, backed with Andrews' instantly forgettable "Ya-Ya-Da-Da", and released as a single in July 1964. The record received little airplay, and did not chart, but the producer of *Ready, Steady, Go!* liked it, and invited her on to the show. The A-side was as good as most of the others penned by Andrew, but was marketed at the wrong time. Had Sandie recorded it a later down the track, it might have proved a hit. Pye therefore urged Eve Taylor to drop

Sandie and concentrate on her other acts: instead, Taylor opted to play on the Adam Faith connection. It is not known if he and Sandie were ever romantically involved, but to have her riding on his coat-tails, so to speak, was no bad thing so far as Taylor was concerned. Though she had deliberated, initially, the wily manager knew when she was onto a good thing.

Andrews and Sandie developed an unconventional way of working together. He composed a melody, which he presented to Sandie. Sometimes there would be a rough lyric but often he left the storyline to her, and she frequently chose an episode from her own life. "I was close to her, so I knew what she was going through—if she's had an unhappy love affair, for instance," he told *History of Rock* in 1982, whilst she responded in her autobiography, *The World At My Feet*, "We drew on our shared urban angst, purging our pain in song, laughing so much we usually spilt the tea over our notes and had to write the whole thing all over again."

Eve Taylor was barred from the production room, invariably because her interfering presence led to arguments and disrupted the jovial atmosphere. Then, once the song was finished, Andrews handed it to their arranger, most often Ken Woodman, a former trumpeter with the marines. Only then was it sent to Taylor. Effectively, most of these songs were joint collaborations, with Sandie also doubling as producer, though Taylor would not allow her name to be added to the production credits, believing that *she* would be accused by her rivals of "penny-pinching" by not employing a legitimate producer!

Some of these early songs saw Chris Andrews emulating his idols, Gerry Goffin and Carole King. Another source of inspiration was West Indian music. Andrews performed regularly at the Flamingo or the Bag O' Nails Club where audiences were 90 per cent black, and calypso was the order of the day. In these days before political correctness, Sandie was permitted to perform the genre along with the best of them—today, she would probably find herself accused of poking fun at an ethnic minority which, of course, like Peggy Lee with cod-Hispanic songs such as "Manana", she never did. Andrews is on record as saying that Sandie Shaw was more professional than Cilla, Marianne, Lulu, *and* Petula Clark.

"She had a much purer voice, although Dusty Springfield's records were probably much better produced," he told *History of Rock*, "The people behind her were spending much more time in the studio than we were."

This may be true regarding Sandie's studio work, though it could be argued that no one possessed a purer voice at the time than Marianne Faithfull. And whereas Dusty would spend hours if not days perfecting a song so that the best take could be spliced into the recording by technicians, Sandie more often than not laid down a track in a single take, two or three at the most, but only if someone else slipped up. This had its advantages—an artiste cannot keep stopping and starting during a live performance and justifiably be regarded as professional—though there would be occasions, such as whilst recording her debut album, when the odd retake would not have gone amiss.

Because she started out with a regular songwriter who knew exactly what sort of material suited her best, Sandie never saw the other Brit Girls as rivals and rarely commented on them at the time. "Dusty used to frighten me," she said in a later *Mojo* interview with Lucy O'Brien. "I never knew what to say to her. She seemed so much older and more sophisticated than me....She was a real one-off." Cilla, she said, was "an impassioned *chanteuse*" who had been "a bit of a frump" until coming down to London and been given a new haircut and more fashionable clothes. "I have this image of her," she added. ""Lit by a single spot, belting out heavy duty ballads, her pale skinny arms stretching up and out from her sleeveless long frocks like branches from a tree." Lulu was another matter. "Lulu I didn't get on with too much," she told O'Brien, "Everything I did, she copied. You'd sing with some lefty group or something, she'll sing with some lefty group. You'd to a TV series, she'll do a TV series. And if you design dresses, she'll go with Freemans. It's kind of—*get off*, Lulu!" Kathy Kirby she regarded as "more of a turn-on for our dads," while she appears to have had nothing to say at all about Marianne. She also believed that her aptitude at singing in foreign languages and adapting to European culture put her at an advantage over her rivals. "It saved me from the winter pantos and summer seasons at the end of the pier, for which I am eternally grateful," she said, "The role of *La Grande Dame* has always suited me more than that of Aladdin tights."

The working relationship between Sandie and Eve Taylor was an uneasy one. Surviving, candidly-filmed footage of Taylor discussing "business" with her clients, including Sandie, reveals her to have been a vulgar, tough but fair taskmaster. Indeed, several of these have since her death denounced her in no uncertain terms for being completely tactless. So long as the money was coming in, Taylor never worried herself about the working conditions or what she had to say about anyone.

Sandie remarked of Taylor's tendency to dispatch acts to political hotspots, "She had no idea about wars and revolution: her knowledge of social unrest stopped at the Harrods sale."

Yet few of these artistes wanted to leave her, even when propositioned with better management deals. Taylor was the ultimate control freak who expected nothing but the best from her stars—the biggest of these when Sandie joined their ranks was crooner Val Doonican—and Taylor reciprocated by going to inordinate lengths to protect them, even buying off reporters when there was the slightest whiff of a scandal. She kept a tight rein on finances, ensuring that no one ever went overboard with expenditure.

"It was she who knew how to do those mysterious things like pay bills, write invoices, haggle over prices and—the ultimate mystery—write cheques," Sandie recalled. "Although I was earning fortunes I just had pocket money and a clothes allowance. Eve opened up accounts for me everywhere....I just walked into shops, ordered things, and the bills were somehow paid."

If Taylor believed that an artiste had something to offer, she would barge relentlessly through any obstacles blocking their path to get them the best deal. Also, she was not averse to stepping on a few toes. In the wake of the failed single, Taylor flew to

Los Angeles where, pretending to be looking for material for Adam Faith, she infiltrated the Burt Bacharach camp. As had happened with "Anyone Who Had A Heart" and several other songs, it was the luckless Dionne Warwick who provided another Brit Girl with the breakthrough she had been looking for. Bacharach had earmarked "Always Something There To Remind Me", a minor hit for Lou Johnson earlier in the year, for Warwick. The subject—a woman revisiting the haunt where she once walked with her former lover—was essentially for an older singer and like Marianne's "As Tears Go By", would not come into its own other than as a pop song until a few years later, when Sandie re-recorded it, and Peggy Lee covered it. The composers, of course, were not interested in who sang it so long as it brought in the "readies" and Eve Taylor was of the same opinion when she heard Warwick rehearsing it—she promptly nabbed it for Sandie! There was a potential hitch when Bacharach announced that the trombone introduction and the unusual key-changes, ranging over two octaves, could not be changed: no problem for Sandie, who recorded it two days after her manager returned to London. Her "late night" version of the song, arranged by classical musician Les Williams, was released in September 1964. Sandie performed it on *Ready, Steady, Go!* and on Jack Good's *Shindig*. Within two weeks it topped the British charts where it stayed for three weeks, ousting Roy Orbison's "Pretty Woman", though it only reached Number 52 in the US charts. Chris Andrews' "Don't You Know", which like so many of her early songs has Sandie addressing somebody else's lover as opposed to her own, was on the flipside.

Dionne Warwick would have to wait three years before recording "Always Something There To Remind Me", but played alongside Sandie's full-bodied, emotive interpretation, her reading sounds empty and dull. Sandie re-recorded it years later for the soundtrack of the film, *Letter To Brezhnev*. In France, Ralph Bernel came up with an almost word-for-word translation for Eddie Mitchell: "Toujours un coin qui me rappelle" shot to the top of the French charts, though compared to Sandie's version (where she retains the title but sings "Toujours *ce* coin", meaning that this was not just any old haunt, but a special one!) Mitchell's was flat and tuneless. During the same session Sandie also recorded "Ne crois pas", the French adaptation of "Don't You Know". Over the years, she would cover most of her hits phonetically in French, and be able to command the talents of such distinguished lyricists as Jean-Max Riviere and Gérard Bourgeois, who worked regularly with Juliette Gréco—but unlike the German, Italian and Spanish adaptations, few were lyrically related to the originals.

A heated argument with Eve Taylor saw the wily manager hitting on another gimmick for Sandie's third single, released in November. The two chosen songs were "I'd Be Far Better Off Without You" and "Girl Don't Come", both by Chris Andrews. The latter, another late night number with a trombone introduction similar to that of "Always Something There To Remind Me", tells of the girl who fails to turn up for a date with a friend. It was initially devised as a ballad and was Sandie's choice for the A-side—until Taylor decided that it required speeding up. Sandie therefore switched her affection to the other song. In the end, seven days before the record was scheduled for release, Sandie performed both songs on a late-night chat show and fans were asked to phone in with their preference for the A-side. They plumped for "Girl Don't Come", and a few days later this was promoted on *Ready, Steady, Go!* Pye forecast that it would become that year's Christmas Number One, but it stalled at Number 3.

In February 1965 Sandie released her debut album, simply entitled *Sandie*. Adhering to the same trend as her contemporaries, this comprised a mixture of pop, standards, essential covers of American hits, and a dash of Motown. The sleeve-notes observed:

> As a Barefoot Princess of Pop, with Adam Faith as her personal Prince Charming, the angularly beautiful girl, with her intuitive 'feel' for a good song, has become one of the most exciting vocal discoveries in years.

There was, however, precious little "intuitive feel": as had happened with Cilla Black's debut album, the powers that be (in Sandie's case, Eve Taylor) chose material unsuited to her voice. Like Cilla, in her lower range she can be unbelievably tender—sexy, even—but as soon as she begins mounting the scales, raucousness sets in. Thankfully this situation would improve substantially, and rapidly so. Things get off to a shaky start with the opener, "Everybody Loves A Lover", the one that started it all—though if this version is anything to go by, she might have been better off leaving it behind at the Ilford Palais.

136

Much of it is sung off-key, and by attempting the Motown sound, even with Les Williams' otherwise excellent saxophone solo, the whole thing ends up a mess. Her R & B take on "Gotta See My Baby Every Day" is on the other hand a vast improvement on the original, written by Chris Andrews for Adam Faith. Great too is Victor Young's "Love Letters", even though Sandie appears to be emulating Dionne Warwick—better, it may be said, than Warwick herself. A second Adam Faith number, "Stop Feeling Sorry For Yourself", is amazing—a few more up-tempo numbers like this, alternating with the ballads, and the album would have proved overall definitive instead of just so-so. Again, Sandie encounters no problem by not changing the gender of the lyrics. She *almost* ruins another firm favourite, Irving Berlin's "Always", by rushing through the opening stanza like a high-speed train, but is saved by the female backing singers who, whilst corny, give the piece a nice late-Forties effect. Then it is back to the mediocre as she closes Side One with an effort to out-shrill Cilla at her most strident: "Don't Be That Way" was one of two songs on the album written by Chris Andrews, and not one he should have been proud of.

Side Two of *Sandie* kicks off with a corker: her take on Betty Everett's "It's In His Kiss" is classier than the original, and the same could almost be said for "Downtown"—Petula Clark's version may just have had the edge, not on account of her vocals but because of the superior orchestral arrangement. Had Sandie's version been put out as a single instead of "Girl Don't Come", Petula might have had very serious chart competition. The excellence continues with the foot-stomping "You Won't Forget Me", from the pen of Jackie DeShannon. Next up is Will Holt's "Lemon Tree", based on the Portuguese *fado*, "Meu limao, meu limoero", popularised during the late-Thirties. On radio request programmes such as *Children's Favourite*, Sandie's Harry Belafonte-style calypso interpretation of this was the perfect companion piece to Cilla's "Liverpool Lullaby". Then the quality depreciates with a cover of The Four Tops' "Baby I Need Your Loving", which sees Sandie veering off course until she loses direction completely. The album closes with Chris Andrews' "Talk About Love"—this last number the Sandie Shaw the fans would come to know and love, Sixties Brit-Pop at its best and least-complicated.

The album reached Number 3 in the charts, in what was a one-off achievement. Commercially, Sandie would remain a singles artiste, and once the sales of these diminished, so too did the sales of her albums—primarily because, the more independent she became, the less adept she was at choosing material which suited her. Meanwhile, she had Eve Taylor to select and advise, and coinciding with the album's release was Sandie's fourth single, Chris Andrews' "I'll Stop At Nothing", coupled with his "You Can't Blame Him". Andrews had written this for Adam Faith, about to embark on a nationwide tour, but in the dog-eat-dog music world, with Faith's career on the slide while Sandie's was very much in its ascendency, Eve Taylor gave the song to her—and included her in the tour, which must have been a daunting decision for Faith, who now learned that he had been demoted to supporting act. The record peaked at Number 4 in the charts.

138

The tour kicked off on 21 February 1965—five days before Sandie turned eighteen, at Leicester's De Montfort Hall. Here she stumbled over her opening number, but put this down to first night nerves. After that it was plain sailing, though as the tour progressed Adam Faith found his popularity threatened as Sandie's fans clamoured for more: over the course of the next few months, as the package zipped up and down the country, new dates were added at the last minute. The Paramounts, an outfit from Southend who had a minor hit with "Poison Ivy", should have had their own spot, but Eve Taylor relegated them to Sandie's backing group, bringing criticism from the *New Musical Express*, who accused her of reducing a fine band of musicians into "a faceless unit just there to back a famous pop singer."

The magazine castigated Sandie for pausing at the end of her set to thank Adam Faith, The Barron Knights, and everyone else involved with the tour *except* The Paramounts. The black "Rescue Me" singer Fontella Bass, who supported, accused her of treating her musicians with contempt—in reference to her "no birds and booze in the dressing room" decree while touring, which on the face of it seemed a reasonable request. It took Sandie until February 1966 to respond to Bass's comment, posing the question, "*She* said that? The immigrant?"—earning herself no plaudits from the music press.

Sandie was unique among the Brit Girls in that, when she covered a man's song, she rarely changed the lyrics. Thus she would eventually sing, "I'll stop at nothing, until I get the girl I love." She appears to have done this in April 1965 during a trip to Canada

139

—the record was in the lower reaches of the charts there. Depending on the province, she performed in English or French, a language she initially sang in phonetically, until she became more adept. She still had a marked English accent, and like most non-French performers—Joséphine Baker and Petula Clark especially—she always encountered problems with the words *tu* and *du*, pronouncing these *too* and *doo*, which caused no little confusion when she was singing songs such as "Pourvu que ca dure", the French adaptation of "Long Live Love." Over the next few years she recorded extensively in French, German, Italian and Spanish—firstly covers of her hits then, as her popularity increased, original songs. Effectively she had more chart hits on the Continent than in Britain. "Domani," the Italian adaptation of "Tomorrow", sold over a million copies, and another big hit at the time was Gianni Marchetti's "Guardo te che te ne vai", which Sandie never sang in English.

From Canada, Sandie should have crossed the border into the United States, where she had been booked for Ed Sullivan's *Talk Of The Town* television show. Sullivan, a hugely influential figure but renowned in the trade for his moral stance and rudeness to guests, had been sent a copy of "Girl Don't Come"—save that a misprint on the record label read, "Girls Don't Come". This, and the rumour that Sandie sometimes perform "cross-gender" songs, made him see red. Not only did he refuse to have her on his show, he got his producer to report her to the appropriate authorities so that she was denied a work-permit to perform in America. A subsequent expletives-laden telephone call from Eve Taylor soon saw this lifted: Sandie was still not permitted to appear on the Sullivan programme, but she did briefly tour the country. In 1994 she told John Naughton of the *Observer* of the printing error which had led to the ban, "Well, I'd much rather have that claim to fame than licking America's arse, which a lot of people did."

Meanwhile, "Long Live Love", Chris Andrew's calypso mini-masterpiece which he claimed he had written in five minutes flat, rocketed to the top of the British charts. To Tony Hatch's dismay it ousted his girlfriend (later his wife) Jackie Trent's "Where Are You Now?" from the top slot, and was unseated by Elvis Presley's "Crying In The Chapel"—but while they only stayed at the top one week each, Sandie spent three weeks there. As "Pourvu que ca dure" it reached the Top 10 in France. In accepting the song, Eve Taylor had on her behalf rejected "It's Not Unusual", which gave Tom Jones a Number One. Later, Sandie claimed that *she* had turned down the song, telling John Naughton, "I mean, *I* didn't need it. I had people giving me songs left, right and centre and it was obviously tailor-made for him. They were trying to give it to a big star so it would be guaranteed to get into the charts."

"Long Live Love" was a hit in Holland, Germany and Scandinavia. Sandie toured Europe extensively during the Sixties and towards the end of the decade when sales dipped in the UK, she would still be selling millions of records across the Channel. The French, following her three-week run at the Paris Olympia in October 1965, when she and The Paramounts supported Richard Anthony, nicknamed her "La chanteuse aux pieds nus". She later claimed

141

that she had stolen the show from Anthony, and that he had asked her to remove "Always Something There To Remind Me" from her set because *he* was singing this in French. Neither is true: Anthony was a huge star in France, and when erroneously informed a few weeks before the premiere that *Cilla* would be supporting him, he had requested that she not sing "You're My World" which he had recorded several months before her. It was Eddie Mitchell who had covered the Sandie song.

Sandie admired the great French singers—Piaf, Aznavour, Gréco—not just for their work, but for the way they had been treated with respect by the media, as opposed to the way the British press treated *its* stars. "They don't do what we do—set them on a pedestal, then start throwing things at them," she told BBC London radio in September 2008, "They really embrace them, particularly the women." Her claims that she had worked with Piaf and Jacques Brel were however entirely false. Piaf's final performances had taken place in Paris in February 1963, eight months before her death, which occurred around the time Sandie was making her amateur stage debut in Ilford—and, aside from Marlene Dietrich, Brel was only ever supported by French singers between 1964 and his retirement from live performances four years later.

After the Olympia, Sandie went on tour with rocker Johnny Hallyday. Marlene Dietrich invited her to guest on her Berlin television during one of only two returns to her homeland since her self-imposed exile in the wake of Hitler's rise to power.

"It was to show there were no hard feelings after what she'd said about my friend, Piaf," Marlene told me—though she never elaborated on this, only that a small group of enraged Piaf fans had set fire to some of Sandie's albums outside the Gare du Nord station, as they had done with Cilla's "Love Of The Loved" when Brian Epstein had boasted, just weeks after Piaf's death and when the whole of France had been in mourning, that *his* star would become *bigger* than Piaf.

Sandie is believed to have been the "mystery" singer who joins in with the chorus on "Fur alles kommt die Zeit", Marlene's cover of The Byrds' "Turn, Turn, Turn". America, however, she would never conquer, nor apparently want to, much preferring to stick to the countries where she felt she was the most appreciated.

With Adam Faith.

2: Nothing Less Than Brilliant

Like Marianne, primarily on account of her stunning looks, high cheekbones, long glossy black hair and statuesque figure, Sandie found herself courted by some of Europe's most distinguished film directors, including Federico Fellini and Franco Zeffirelli. Mostly these wanted her for cameos, though Fellini is on record as saying he could have turned her into a new Greta Garbo—nonsense, of course, for Garbo will never be replaced. Czech-born Karel Reisz, famed for *Saturday Night And Sunday Morning* (1960) and *This Sporting Life* (1963) approached her with an unspecified role—and ended up directing her in a television commercial for Lux soap! "They asked me not to sing," Sandie says in the 30-seconds film and, nestling her bare feet in a sheepskin rug, concludes of the product, "It makes me feel good all over, right down to my toes!"

Next, she was courted by Cy Endfield, who had directed *Zulu* (1964). Endfield offered her third lead in an unnamed film with future one-off James Bond actor George Lazenby, which Eve Taylor urged her to accept—until she learned that she would be expected to do a near-nude love scene.

"Maybe they wanted to save on wardrobe expenses," she joked, adding of the several similar roles she rejected, "As I knew they would be less than impressed with my credentials, I proved an extremely reluctant movie queen."

Eve Taylor was approached by Tommy Steele's management with a request for Sandie to star opposite him in the film version of *Half A Sixpence*, and less importantly to appear with Peter Noone, of Herman's Hermits', in *Mrs. Brown You've Got A Lovely Daughter*. Both were turned down.

In September 1966, Pye released Chris Andrew's catchy "Message Understood", c/w "Don't You Count On It". Eve Taylor had been in favour of Sandie recording his "Yesterday Man", but for once she put her foot down and refused to have anything to do with the idea, declaring that she disliked the melody. Andrews recorded it himself in a squeaky, not very endearing voice—but took it to Number 2 in the charts, his one and only hit, while "Message Understood" stalled at Number 6.

Sandie's second album, *Me*, was released in November and failed to chart, giving Eve Taylor the impression that maybe her protégée was heading in the same direction as Helen Shapiro and Kathy Kirby. Even so, it was far better and more consistent than its predecessor and may even be considered a *great* album: with this one there is no hit and miss regarding quality—*all* the songs are excellent, the covers as good as if not superior to the originals. It opens with Charles Blackwell's Continental-style ballad, "You Don't Love Me No More". Previously a hit for Madeleine Bell, it is way too short but sufficient to tickle the taste-buds and prepare the listener for what is to come. "I Don't Need That Kind Of Loving", heavy on the guitars, and with Sandie appearing to emulate "My Boy Lollipop" singer Millie Small is nevertheless above the regular Chris Andrews breezy-pop fare—the first of his six compositions here. This leads nicely into his "Down Dismal Ways", the perfect R & B vehicle for showcasing Sandie's two-and-a-half octave range—

the French version of this, "La vallée des larmes", is amazing. Great fun is "Oh No He Don't", her calypso duet with Andrews which would have made a superb single. Sandie even jokes at the end when she asks Andrews, "You *think* I get Harry Belafonte next time?" Next up, and a distinct change of pace, is Mark McIntyre and Floyd Huddleston's "When I Was A Child", written for Peggy Lee and included on her 1961 *If You Go* album. The simplistic but effective lyrics are based on a passage from *Corinthians*. Peggy is on record as saying that she really liked this one: in 1970 this mutual admiration would be reciprocated when Peggy recorded a near-definitive cover of "Always Something There To Remind Me" for her *Bridge Over Troubled Water* album, while two years after this, Sandie recorded Peggy's "Where Did They Go?" Side One of *Me* ends with Lionel Bart's "Do You Mind?" sung in tongue-in-cheek Cockney argot. Anthony Newley had performed the original.

Side Two gets off to a cracking start with Jimmy Williams and Larry Harrison's "How Good I Am", formerly a hit for Nancy Wilson. Others had covered this, but none so adeptly as Sandie. Brimming with even more profound optimism is "I Know", reminiscent of Edith Piaf's "Les neiges de Finlande" where Sandie juxtaposes happy childhood memories of fairy tales, lemonade mountains and chocolate fountains but with a portentous warning for the future: for if one cannot be happy when young, one might never be happy again! Then comes her own composition, "Till The Night Begins To Die"—pretty innovative for a first effort, and much better than some of the material she wrote for

146

herself later in her career. The same may not be said for Chris Andrews' "Too Bad You Don't Want Me", which begs the question—who exactly is Sandie mimicking here in this raucous piece of neo-Fats Domino nonsense, which would have been better omitted from the album altogether? Then, from the ridiculous to the sublime, we have "One Day", not just the best track on the album, but one the finest songs Andrews ever composed. The subject is the precognitive dream—the fact that all will turn out well if this is what one wishes. The man must go away, but though it breaks her heart to say goodbye, the woman is confident that they will meet again and rekindle their dreams and aspirations. In the meantime, she will survive on the happy memories, and all that she asks in return is that he think about her from time to time. It is a mini-masterpiece which might have been better off closing the album, rather than Sandie's take on the Nat King Cole classic, "When I Fall In Love", which could have been improved on, had Ken Woodman taken a little more time working on the arrangement. Sandie sings if way too fast—it and she deserve better than the cheap-sounding "musak" backing.

Pye played on Fellini's "Garbo" quote by housing the new album in a sleeve containing a stunning monochrome portrait by Michael Williams—an extreme close-up of Sandie's face which highlighted her angular cheekbones and beautiful eyes. The reason her eyes looked so languid, she said, was because she was so incredibly short-sighted: she was not joking when, during her first appearance on *Juke Box Jury*, a technician asked her to look at Camera Two and she replied that she could not even

147

see it! Eve Taylor was wrong in promoting *Me* as an album of cabaret songs—and she made an even bigger mistake, pulling the requisite strings to book Sandie for three weeks at the Savoy Hotel. With a programme almost exclusively of Chris Andrews material, she opened at the beginning of November. Andy Gray of the *New Musical Express* observed:

> Barefooted—yet looking stunning with her glossy black hair, her pinkish dress with bolero top and skirt swinging freely—she just wasn't experienced enough for the gigantic ordeal of opening at the Savoy Hotel cabaret, but top marks for trying.

Sandie's initial dilemma was a combination of bad nerves and a weak (for this environment) repertoire. Andrews may have been a more than competent composer of pop songs, but he was not a writer for the cabaret circuit. Also, to have Sandie backed by The Paramounts and not the hotel's resident orchestra, turning the event in "just another pop concert" was another grave error on Taylor's part.

The opening night was a near disaster. Sandie's set was exactly the same as it had been during the tour. She forgot the words to her opening song, "That's Where It Is", and dried up completely during "I'll Stop At Nothing". After two more attempts at this, she shouted to The Paramounts, "Forget it!", then laughed off her gaff, telling the audience that this had always been her unlucky song. A few songs later, she cursed aloud because she had splinters in her feet—a problem which the Savoy management rectified during the rest of her season by sanding the stage before she went on. Her feet caused "distress" for the upper-crust clientele, who complained that it was inappropriate to have an artiste on stage, minus her shoes, while they were eating! After reading one not so impressive review of the opening night, Eve Taylor stepped in: the shoes stayed off, but the Andrews songs were swapped for recognisable standards like "Lemon Tree" and "Always". The Paramounts were replaced by the Streamliners. Soon afterwards, they disbanded and three of their members—lead guitarist Robin Trower, bassist Chris Copping, and vocalist Gary Brooker—went on to better things when they joined Procul Harum.

The Shaw-Andrews partnership suffered a setback at the end of the year when Sandie's single of his "How Can You Tell?" an upbeat, cha-cha number stalled at Number 21 in the charts. This, and the failure of *Me* (one must remember that at this time, pop success was measured in record sales) almost tempted Eve Taylor to find Sandie another songwriter. She gave Andrews another chance, and he came up with "Tomorrow", and this restored them to their former glory, peaking at Number 10 in the charts in February 1966. Taylor cancelled any plans she had for Sandie recording a third album, and to keep the fans happy, Pye put out *The Golden Hits Of Sandie Shaw* on its budget Marble Arch label. This contained her 1964-5 singles and their B-sides. Seven were Chris Andrews compositions, but as diehard fans already had this material, the album did not chart. This year too there were more EP mini-compilations released than would normally have been expected: none of them charted, but they sold enough to keep the royalties coming in.

Inasmuch as Eve Taylor had "kicked herself" for rejecting "It's Not Unusual", so she would rue turning down Burt Bacharach's "Alfie" in favour of Chris Andrew's "Nothing Comes Easy", which reached Number 14 in the charts during the early summer. The subject is stalking. Despite the scheming to find the perfect lover, once she has ensnared him, she realises that the thrill was only in the chase, and that she does not want him any more—and now, she must pay the price for being so possessive because he follows her everywhere, and will not leave her alone. The Italian adaptation stormed to the top of the charts there, and at the end of June, Sandie headed for Venice, where she participated in the International Song Festival before recording a new clutch of songs (including original compositions) in Italian for a proposed album. These were subsequently relegated to a series of extended singles: all of them charted. The Italian tabloids also reported an incident when, backstage at the festival, Sandie found herself surrounded by a large group of lothario male fans. When one of these pinched her bottom, she rounded on him—only to punch the wrong man on the nose! "He must have been under the impression that this was the English way of reciprocating appreciation," she later mused. Far from wanting to take action against his idol, the man declared that being "floored" by Sandie Shaw would remain the happiest moment of his life!

Another incident took place in Palermo, Italy, where Sandie had been engaged to sing at a nightclub. She was approached by a Mafioso businessman who offered to up her fee considerably

150

should she agree to sing at *his* club. Eve Taylor very rarely accompanied her artistes on overseas tours, and was not present to sort out the mess when Sandie refused his offer. The man, who appears to have had the local police in his pocket, exacted his revenge by instructing them to swoop on the beach where Sandie and her party were sunbathing, confiscate everyone's passports, and impound their fees which Taylor had insisted should be paid up-front. The items would then be duly returned once Sandie had completed her "obligation". Sandie, forewarned, claimed she had hidden the passports in her bikini, and to have handed the money to one of her musicians, who buried it in the sand. The police still confiscated everyone's clothes, and that evening everyone was obliged to perform in their swimwear! The next day, Eve Taylor flew out to Italy, bought everything back from the police, and returned the party home.

Sandie's next UK single was Chris Andrews' "Run"—in the days before promotional videos an allegorical piece which begins with a thunderclap and a curious, Arab-style introduction. The song deals with the paranoia of a woman unable to let her lover go. She sees him everywhere and relates these sightings to the weather: the wind is *him* calling her, the rain is *him* following her, the sun is *his* shadow. She dare not answer the door, or telephone—all she can do is keep on running. In France, this became "L'orage", with the storm occupying centre stage. Though the record reached Number 32 in the charts, Pye declared it her worst-selling release since "As Long As You're Happy, Baby"—again sales were put before lyrical and musical excellence. Andrews'

"Think Sometimes About Me", released in November, attained the same chart position: the flipside, "Hide All Emotion", was written especially for Sandie by Marty Wilde.

From its dramatic opening through to the crescendo which precedes its stupendous climax, "I Don't Need Anything"—Sandie's first single of 1967—sounds like the kind of Italian ballad one would expect from Dusty or Cilla. It is in fact an American impersonation of the genre—and a good one at that—by Lee Pockriss and Paul Vance. The flipside, Chris Andrews' "Keep In Touch", was almost as good—this adopted the same calypso formula as "Long Live Love", with each stanza progressively getting shorter and broken up by a series of sharp, musical interludes. It received very little airplay, and only reached Number 50 in the charts. By now, Pye obviously no longer considered Sandie a major commercial draw and their response to the record's failure was to shelve plans for her next album, as had happened before, and to put out the compilation, *Sandie Sings*, on their mid-price Golden Guinea label. Then, early in the New Year, everything changed when Sandie was asked to represent the United Kingdom in the Eurovision Song Contest, be held on 8 April in Vienna, at the Burghof, the former Hapsburg winter residence. Her initial response was a very firm, "No!"

"Visions of hairy-legged Scotsmen warbling jolly ditties....dotty duos trilling birdie songs came to mind," she said, in reference to previous United Kingdom entrants Kenneth McKellar and Teddie Johnson and Pearl Carr.

The BBC and Eve Taylor persuaded her to change

her mind. The ensuing publicity of her participating in "Euroyawn", as she scathingly referred to it, would they hoped prevent the divorce scandal in which Sandie had recently become embroiled from hitting the press. 27-year-old Duncan Murdoch had worked as a production assistant on *Ready, Steady, Go!* He and Sandie had apparently been dating for a while, and Murdoch had asked her to marry him— without letting on that he was still married. His wife, Veronica, had cited Sandie as correspondent. Taylor was given additional incentive to "persuade" her star to enter the contest: one of the BBC executives informed her that unless Sandie co-operated, Taylor risked being blacklisted—a move which effectively could have seen *all* of her artistes banned from appearing on the BBC television and radio networks.

Everyone involved with the contest was confident that she *would* win Eurovision hands-down because, of all the entries being submitted that year, she was by far the biggest star, having sold over 40 million records in Europe. Indeed, throughout the whole of 1967 there was not one European country which did *not* have a Sandie Shaw record in its Top Ten. Two years later, much fuss would be made of the contest being "fixed" to enable General Franco's favourite, Massiel, to win for Spain. 1967 was little different, but all above board. "Putting Sandie Shaw into that contest was like entering Red Rum in a one-horse Grand National," Dorothy Squires said.

In the run-up to the public vote, Sandie performed one of the five shortlisted songs each week on the BBC's *The Rolf Harris Show*: "Ask Any Woman", Tell The Boys", "I'll Cry Myself To Sleep", "Had A

Dream Last Night", and "Puppet On A String".
Once she got used the idea of participating, her
favourite song was Pete Callander's and Mitch
Murray's "Tell The Boys", but the viewers decided
otherwise and chose the one she disliked, Phil
Coulter and Bill Martin's "Puppet On A String".

"I hated it from the first oompah to the final bang
on the big bass drum," she said. "Even in those
days, before the phrase 'chauvinist pig' had been
coined, I was instinctively repelled by its sexist
drool and cuckoo-clock tune."

The "oompah" idea derived from Sandie's
popularity in Germany. Later she said how she
would have rather lost the contest with a song she
loved than win it with one she could not stand.

Sandie flew to Vienna with a 30-strong British
delegation which included Eve Taylor, Adam Faith,
Rolf Harris and their spouses, her parents, arranger
Ken Woodman, and numerous BBC and Pye
executives. The whole exercise was reported to
have been a non-stop row with everyone at each
other's throats.

"When I walked on the stage, no one was talking
to me," she told *The Observer Music Monthly*, forty
years after the event. "So the Essex girl in me came
out, and I did it on my own, 'Fuck you', it's one of
those. Needless to say, they all wanted to speak to
me afterwards."

As universally forecast, she won the contest, a
first for Britain, way ahead of Sean Dunphy, who
came second for Ireland. She attracted adverse
criticism from some of the participating countries
who accused the judges of being biased towards her
because if her popularity in Europe. She had already

recorded "Puppet On A String" in five languages, and in Germany there were 500,000 advance orders for the single. The lyrics for the French version had been commissioned from Pierre Delanoe, who had written numerous million-sellers for Edith Piaf. It was an incredible song all the same, and despite a microphone failure which meant her having to start again, Sandie gave an exemplary performance. It was not however the most commercially successful song that year—this honour went to Paul Mauriat's "Love Is Blue", performed for Luxembourg by Vicky Leandros, who came fourth. Sandie's single, backed with "Tell The Boys", shot to the top of the UK charts, and was a massive hit in just about every country in Europe. Yet despite her professing not to like the song, for another twenty years, each time she stepped on to a stage, she would be expected to sing it—indeed, as her biggest selling recording, it would be her duty to do so.

Sandie disapproved of the way the BBC's Terry Wogan handled the commentary for Eurovision, the fact that for nigh on thirty years, and on a reputed exorbitant fee he had rarely had a non-cynical thing to say about any aspect of the contest. The songs, the singers, and the way they dressed all came up for ultra-sarcastic scrutiny which Sandie believed to be decidedly anti-European. Speaking to the *Times'* Tim Teeman in May 2007, the year before Wogan stepped down, she fumed:

> He takes the piss out of them. I don't know how much time he spends in Europe, but if he did he would know how lucky those people were and he *wouldn't* take the bloody

piss out of them. I love them for their sense of fun, their sense of can do. They're not like English people. Whatever situation they're in, they will find a way to enjoy it.

On 26 February 2007, on the occasion of her sixtieth birthday, Sandie re-released the song on her website. "Puppet's Got A Brand New String" was given a new arrangement by Howard Jones and Andy Gray—slow and sultry, it was not a patch on the original and sounded like some half-hearted effort from a tired boy band.

"It was [Jones] idea to re-record it, to cure me," she told *Observer Music Monthly*, "He just made me sing it in a different way. I know it sounds strange, but it's been like therapy. I'm at peace with it now."

Some things, however, could *never* be improved upon!

Eurovision '67 ended with an amusing incident which took place at Vienna airport. Eve Taylor, who had treated everyone with disdain during the trip, now could not praise Sandie enough. When she saw the long queue at customs, grabbing hold of Sandie's arm she ushered her to the front. Here, a young customs official lightheartedly remarked, "Go to the back of the queue, madame. She's not the Queen of England, yet,"—at which Taylor growled, "Actually, that's where you're fucking wrong, mate. Right now, she *is* the Queen of England!"

With her Svengali manager, Eve Taylor.

Looking Garboesque on the sleeve of *Me*.

A German album cover featuring Sandie &
Chris Andrews.

Eurovision 67, with previous
year's winner Udo Jurgens.

3: Reviewing The Situation

Pye, who had almost given up on Sandie, rush-released an album in the wake of her Eurovision victory, also titled *Puppet On A String*, while Eve Taylor was bombarded with requests for her to perform all over the world. The album was nothing special for most fans: full-priced, it contained just three new songs—Chris Andrews' "No Moon", "Keep In Touch", and his "I Don't Think You Want Me Anymore", which would be superbly adapted into French by former yé-yé singer Johnny Rech— as "Tout est change", quite possibly Sandie's best ever interpretation in this language. The album also included a re-recording of "I'd Be Far Better Off Without You", yet still failed to chart.

Despite this renewed lack of commercial success, Sandie was still hailed Britain's top female singer, and everyone wanted a piece of the action. Don Short, a *Daily Mirror* columnist, announced that he was writing a biography, while Sandie claimed to be dictating her memoirs, *Little Miss Puppet*, neither of which emerged. Yet despite being in demand on the cabaret circuit the singles moved slowly once "Puppet On A String" dropped out of the charts. Its successor, "Tonight In Tokyo", reached Number 21, while "You've Not Changed" peaked at Number 18.

In October 1967, Pye released *Love Me, Please Love Me*, an album mostly of standards which did not chart, but which may still justifiably be regarded as a work of considerable greatness. The title-track was by French enigma Michel Polnareff, discovered two years earlier by Dalida's husband, Lucienne Morisse, busking on the steps of the Sacre Coeur, in

Paris. Retaining the English title, Polnareff recorded the song in French and it sold a million copies. Sandie adhered to the original arrangement, which requires the singer to jump two octaves in the middle of each stanza. Polnareff had achieved this by launching into vocalese, whereas Sandie, compelled to actually pronounce the words, cleverly drops a tone. The next song, Antonio Carlos Jobim's "One Night Samba", sees her making a valiant attempt as scat—she had been incorporating bits of this into her songs for a while, and like Helen Shapiro was a natural when it came to jazz. Next up is "Smile", and a change of pace for the Charlie Chaplin classic. "Yes, My Darling Daughter", based on a Ukranian folk song and given lyrics by Jack Lawrence, had been reintroduced by Dinah Shore in 1941. Sandie performs it in ragtime. Jacques Brel's "Ne me quitte pas", which she sings throughout in French, is not so enigmatic: Sandie sings it way too fast and in doing so messes up the lyrics somewhat. A retake would not have gone amiss. Side one ends brilliantly, however, with a sterling take on Cole Porter's "Every Time We Say Goodbye", which Ella Fitzgerald had made her own.

Side Two opens with a rip-roaring version of Geoff Stephens' "The Way That I Remember Him", reminiscent of Kathy Kirby's "The Way Of Love". Stephens had written many hits, including "The Crying Game" for Dave Berry. The following year, Dana would win Eurovision with his "All Kinds Of Everything". Next up is "Hold Him Down", another witty calypso by Chris Andrews which, if slightly out of place on this collection, maybe would not have been permitted in today's frequent over-excess of political correctness. Again, Pye might have been better off releasing this as a single, rather than Andrews' "Today" which limped into the charts and stalled at Number 27. Next, Sandie moves into big band territory, firstly with Cole Porter's "I Get A Kick Out Of You", then with Sammy Cahn and Jule Styne's "Time After Time", which has some great saxophone playing from Les Williams. Then, after Chris Andrews' dispensable "That's Why", Sandie rounds off the proceedings with a superlative reading of Howard Dietz and Arthur Schwartz's "By Myself", the Judy Garland showstopper. Whereas Judy piled on the emotion, Sandie aims for a gentler approach—not as effective, but great just the same.

Though immensely popular on the cabaret circuit, from her record company's point of view 1968 proved Sandie's worst year yet—her next five singles all flopped. The most impressive of these was an adaptation of "Dorogoi dlinnoyu", a Russian song dating back to the 1920s. As "Le temps des fleurs", this had recently proved a massive hit in France for Dalida, but long before that there had been an English version, "Those Were The Days", by Gene Raskin. When Eve Taylor learned that *Opportunity Knocks!* winner Mary Hopkin was planning to release this as a single on the Beatles' new Apple label, she rushed Sandie into the studio, declaring that the song should be sung by a "real" singer, as opposed to one who had won a talent contest. Clearly, she had forgotten how Sandie had come into *her* life! Apple responded by placing full-page advertisements in the music press, begging people to listen to both records on the radio and to decide which one they preferred, before rushing off

161

to their nearest record shop. The emphasis naturally was on their own artiste, and despite Sandie introducing the song on *Top Of The Pops*, it was Hopkin's inferior, drawn-out version which topped the charts. Sandie's French-language version, if not a patch on Dalida's, sold well on the Continent.

On a personal level, having survived the divorce scandal, Sandie could not have been happier. On 6 March, she secretly married Welsh-born, London-based fashion designer Jeff Banks, three years her senior, at Greenwich Registry Office. Introduced by Eve Taylor, they been dating for a while. It was Banks who, along with Taylor, had organised a surprise 21st birthday party for Sandie the previous year—at Madame Tussauds, where in a ginger wig and one of his creations she had been photographed with Taylor in the Chamber of Horrors! The caption had read, "Sandie & Her Mother". Neither Sandie's nor Banks' parents were told about the wedding until after it had taken place. The bride, just out of hospital having had minor surgery to remove an abdominal cyst, wore a yellow mini-skirt and matching mackintosh and, as a feeble disguise, the aforementioned ginger wig. The witnesses were two hospital porters. Their secret lasted for all twenty-four hours before they were rumbled by the press.

At around this time, Eve Taylor handed Sandie her "inheritance"—money she had been banking from her earnings, while paying her a weekly allowance. She spent this wisely, paying the deposit on a large Victorian house in Blackheath.

The union with Banks would produce a daughter, Grace, born in 1971, who Sandie would later deem to be her closest friend—the one who in lieu of their

162

of their fathers would hold her hand during the births of her subsequent children. "Probably one of the better ones I've had. I'll never have enough time to thank her for all her love and care," she said. A few months later, aided by Banks, Sandie launched her own range of clothes, accessories and shoes.

In September, the BBC gave Sandie her own television series. *The Sandie Shaw Supplement*, a "situation-travelogue" was a six-part variety show produced by Mel Cornish which saw her (courtesy of Cornish, a former set-designer for *Top of the Pops*) emulating the Dalida format: extending her repertoire by performing songs one might not normally have expected, in unusual settings and frequently wearing over-the-top costumes, as Dalida was doing in television shows across the Channel, but in Sandie's case filmed entirely in monochrome, which made the BBC's press-release confusing:

> The title is intended to suggest the glossy world of colour magazines, one of the most glamorous fantasies of all time....A lyrical film of a beautiful girl riding a horse along the beach; driving a white £12,000 Italian car while wearing a white helmet, white trouser-suit and goggles; running through the sun-streamed woods in slow motion; lolling on a beach wearing a tiny bikini; enjoying a vermouth served by a liveried flunkey floating in the sea.

Obviously, Jeff Banks had much to do with the way Sandie was dressed, like the archetypal rock chick, and not always attractively so, revealing more flesh than might have been considered prudent, hence the series' late evening television slot. The locations were shot in Wales in the early spring, and mostly at the crack of dawn with everyone shivering in the strong wind blowing in from the sea. Sadly, most of the tapes were later wiped by the BBC, allegedly in an act of spite, though why they should have done this was never explained. To date, only two copies (Episodes 2 and 3, discovered in a Far Eastern television station vault) have come to light, along with a few clips from the others.

The first episode, *Eyes, Nose, Mouth & A Heartbeat* (the subject was sex, a word not permitted in the title back then) went out on 10 September. Ahead of Morrissey turning this into an art form, Sandie performed throughout in front of a huge backdrop—of herself. She sang the Rolling Stones' "I Can't Get No Satisfaction"—Keith Altham of the *New Musical Express* described it as "downright wicked"—and in a swift change of pace, "Scarborough Fair", before attacking the Troggs' raunchy "Wild Thing", which did not suit her at all. She rounded off the proceedings with a Tony Hatch medley, three Petula Clark songs which are said *not* to have pleased her rival.

The second episode, *Quicksand*, concerned itself with travel, and opened with "Route 66". Then after showing Dionne Warwick how "Do You Know The Way To San Jose" should be done, Sandie launched into a lengthy medley which opened with Georgie Fame's "Get Away" and ended with a Beatles selection, whilst the camera alternated between her face and the backdrop, and old movie footage depicting antiquated means of transport.

164

Episode Three, *Garlic, Pepper & A Touch Of Salt*, had Sandie singing in Spanish, French, Italian and German—it ended with her descending a mock-up of the Folies-Bergere's celebrated staircase while singing "Le temps des fleurs". In the fourth episode, *Reflections*, she paid homage to some of her favourite female stars including Audrey Hepburn, Diana Ross, Marlene Dietrich in her famous swansdown wrap—and Sandie Shaw! Episode Five, *Sandcastles In The Air*, opened with the Rolling Stones' "19th Nervous Breakdown", a decidedly bad choice, and after a delectable Hans Christian Andersen sketch, Sandie audaciously closed with Cilla's "You're My World". The final episode, *A Large Slice Of Bread*, included Shirley Bassey's "Big Spender", several show tunes, and ended with a version of "By Myself" that Judy herself would have been proud of.

The Sandie Shaw Supplement was not, however, a ratings winner: fans disliked the exterior-filmed aspects of the show, preferring to see their Sandie performing on a stage in front of a microphone, therefore a second series was not commissioned. Twenty years later, with the advent of MTV and the promotional video, things might have turned out differently.

In November, a week after the series ended, Pye released *The Sandie Shaw Supplement* "magazine-album". The back of the sleeve depicted arguably the most unflattering Sandie Shaw photograph ever taken: lying on a beach, uncannily resembling Cher in her later raunchy period, she wears a yellow bikini and lots of cheap jewellery, and the most freakish hairstyle. The image is in complete contrast

165

to the content. Since *Sandie*, each album had been vastly improved upon, and this is as good as it gets, though only six of the twelve songs are from the series. Until recording *Love Me, Please Love Me*, Sandie had been accustomed to performing with just a handful of choice musicians—here, old stalwart Ken Goodman conducts a 30-piece orchestra. The album opens with Bobby Troup's "(Get Your Kicks On) Route 66" which critic Stephen Wright (writing in the sleeve-notes for the CD reissue) described as, "A candidate for *the* performance of Sandie Shaw's career." It is a noisy but lively affair, very big-band Seventies, heavy on the brass and drums, and certainly not for late-night relaxing listening! But it is *good*! Next up is Simon and Garfunkel's "Homeward Bound". In the television show, Sandie had duetted on this with John Walker of the Walker Brothers—like Cilla and Dusty, she never really let herself go singing with someone else and this lovely piece, far superior to the original with Sandie's breathy, tone-perfect two-octave vocalising blends exquisitely with the guitars, banjos and backing singers. It alone is well worth the price of the album. Next, she enters the previously unchartered realm of folk. After Marianne and Nana Mouskouri, one instinctively wonders if "Scarborough Fair" could possibly be improved upon. Backed by a single acoustic guitar, and keeping well within her lower register Sandie blends perfectly with the choir and transforms the piece into a *ronde*. Stephen Wright deems her cover of Goffin and King's "Right To Cry" as definitive. Sandie had veered towards their territory with the early Chris Andrews songs but this is the real McCoy: Dusty had *thought*

166

about it, but Sandie just went ahead and did it with tremendous feeling. "How can I ask you to forgive me when I can't even forgive myself?" she asks, and at a time when she was having marriage problems— lamenting the fact that she does not have the right to cry, even though her ex is flaunting his new lover in her face. And to better display what little difference there was between Andrews and the American songwriting duo, his "The Same Thing" comes next, with its unusual but pleasant piano, guitar and cello accompaniment. Side One ends with Bill Martin and Phil Coulter's Italianate lovely, "Our Song Of Love". Written for Engelbert Humperdinck, it was a replacement for "Surround Yourself With Sorrow" (later a hit for Cilla), after Sandie had thankfully turned this horror down.

Side Two opens with the Rolling Stones' "I Can't Get No Satisfaction" the last song one expects to crop up in a Sandie Shaw performance! She sounds rather like an early Suzi Quatro, and this is not good—even worse when one watches the clip from the television show when she performs it wearing just a towel. Was this, Marianne and Stones fans wanted to know, a not so subtle reference to the Redlands scandal? Much has also been discussed over who best puts across the Bee Gees' "Words"— Sandie, Cilla, or the "nanny goat" voice of Robin Gibb. The girls win hands down, but it is impossible to choose one or the other because *both* versions are so very classy. The next track, Chris Andrews' "Remember Me", had been in Sandie's repertoire for some time, but it had taken her until now to get around to recording it. It is a gentle, wistful piece: Peggy Lee considered covering it—only to record a

167

different song with the same title. In 2004 it appeared on ex-Abba singer Agnetha Faltskog's comeback album, *My Colouring Book*. "She has such a special way of singing, and as such is one of my many role models," Faltskog said of Sandie at the time. The next song on the album, Carol Bayer Sager's Motownesque "Change Of Heart", was earmarked for a single, until Pye changed their mind —a good thing, for it is the least impressive song here, a dud amongst so many diamonds.

"Aranjuez, mon amour", adapted from Rodrigo's classical piece, *Concerto de Aranjuez*, had provided Portuguese fado singer Amália Rodrigues with a massive hit across Europe. Sandie retained Amália's arrangement, but she was not permitted to use Guy Bontempelli's lyrics in their entirety—he objected to her singing the line, *"La fleur au coeur, les pieds nus, les pas lents et les yeux éclairés d'un étrange sourire,"* which he claimed would be mistaken by some fans as Sandie drawing attention to her trademark bare feet. As such, she omits the fourth and fifth segments, robbing the piece of its essential meaning—a shame, for hers is the best reading attempted by a British singer. She rounds off the album with another French classic, Gilbert Bécaud's "What Now My Love?"—ploughing through each emotive stanza until she wraps the whole thing up with a staggering, note-perfect cadenza which Bécaud said had brought him to the verge of tears.

Sandie's final hit of the decade—her 21st single— was "Monsieur Dupont". Released in January 1969, this was the English adaptation of the Christian Bruhn song, which tells the story of the girl who goes to Paris for the day, falls for the Gallic charmer and decides she never wants to go home. It had been hit the previous year for German singer Manuela (1943-2001). The single peaked at Number 6 in the charts and also did well in France, where Sandie was reported to have been arrested by a gendarme— for impersonating a gendarme! She was taken to the local commissariat, where the gendarme's superior "fined" her by making her sing the song. The story, in *France-Dimanche*, may or may not have been true, but it made for amusing reading.

In the UK, the successor to "Monsieur Dupont" was "Think It All Over", what Sandie called another "farting oompah" German-style drinking song, and the last of her singles penned by Chris Andrews. It struggled to reach Number 42 in the charts, and would be her last hit for fifteen years. Adapted into French as "Comme un francais", it sounded much better than it did in English.

Shortly after releasing this single, Sandie played a three-weeks season at the London Palladium, sharing the bill with Eve Taylor's other big name, Val Doonican. This was followed by a successful stint at the Talk of The Town. In December she released a self-produced, underground-style album, *Reviewing The Situation*, a complete volte-face for her in that it contained material which, Eve Taylor said, Sandie fans had missed out because they had been too preoccupied with her pop ditties to listen to anything else! For the first time ever, there were no songs by Chris Andrews—in fact, no decent songs at all in an experiment gone woefully wrong. The critics were baffled, and Sandie cannot have thought much of the album either, for in a 1987 interview with *Goldmine* magazine, she forgets how she came to record it. The title-track was from Lionel Bart's *Oliver!* and bad as this is, it is the best thing here. Sandie, tackling Led Zeppelin, could be likened to Maria Callas attempting heavy metal.

Whatever prepossessed Sandie to cover Bob Dylan's "Lay Lady Lay" was explained to Lucy O'Brien during a live discussion for *Mojo* in 2007:

> If you can go into the Tate and admire pictures of beautiful women, naked, why can't I sing about it? So I sang about a beautiful woman on a bed, and for me that was part of the awakening of the feminist thing that was coming up really big in the Seventies.

Whatever her reason, her interpretation sounds just as disappointing as her takes on the Bee Gees' "Sun In My Eyes", Rufus Thomas' "Walking The Dog", and the Lovin' Spoonful's "Coconut Grove", but most especially the Rolling Stones' "Sympathy For The Devil". "This was either a complete misreading of the song, or else a cunning commentary on the conceit of Mick Jagger's satanic pretentions," *Record Collector* observed of the Stones' number. Fans would have to wait another 25 years to hear perhaps the only decent effort from the sessions— Paul McCartney's "Junk", sung *a capella*—along with the deplorable "Frank Mills", from *Hair*, it was added as a bonus track for the CD release. By comparison the French version (allegedly by Johnny Rech, though the tape which emerged in 2002 has no credits for the lyricist) is exceptional.

Fortunately Sandie and most of those who came in

170

contact with her professionally, recognised the error of *Reviewing The Situation*. Over the next three years there would be some excellent singles: Michel Delpech's tribute to the Isle of Wight Festival, "Wight Is Wight" (which she also recorded superbly in French) and which pays homage to Bob Dylan and Donovan, who brought "butterfly rain" to the island; Joe South's "Rose Garden" (which in a repeat of the Mary Hopkin exercise saw her pipped to the post by Lynn Anderson); and Peggy Lee's "Where Did They Go?" were but three. Finally, her contract with Pye came to an end in August 1972 when they released her cover of Cat Stevens' "Father And Son".

With Jeff Banks.

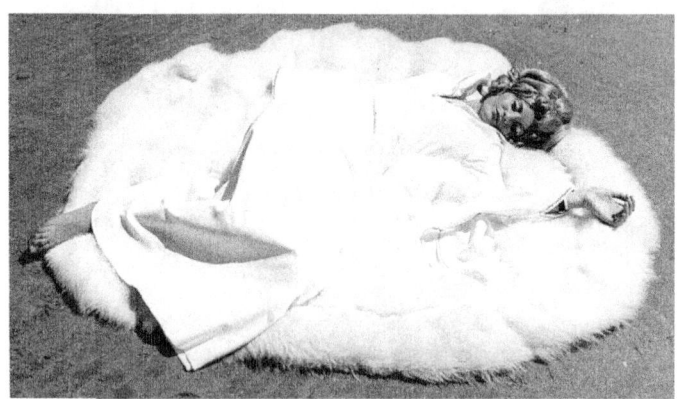

Scenes from *The Sandie Shaw Supplement*.

4: Hand In Glove

As the Seventies dawned, Sandie entered the period she referred to as her "dark ages". Eve Taylor nurtured big hopes of her becoming a family entertainer: chat shows, pantomimes (which Sandie hated), sitcoms, and the like. The divorce scandal had more or less put paid to this—along with the collapse of her marriage to Jeff Banks and their various business ventures, and several lurid tabloid "exclusives" which may or may not have been invented, but which were certainly exaggerated.

"It took us fourteen long, painful, glorious years to grow up, to find out that life was not a game," Sandie reflected. "Losing everything was the best thing that happened to me....my career, my husband, my confidence. I could think, well I've been there. I've been in a deep hole. And once you pull yourself out again it's just incredible."

Nowadays, producers and critics alike would have proved less sensitive but back then—when "family" entertainment meant being given a spot on *The Billy Cotton Band Show* or guesting on *Crackerjack,* as opposed to some "effing and peffing" late night quiz or reality show—things were very different. Singers such as Sandie and Marianne who had "stepped out of line" had no option but to keep on making records or hitting the tour circuit if they wanted their careers to survive. The latter also appears to have presented Sandie with a problem: despite her phenomenal talent, such was her low self-esteem, at times—as will be seen—that she sometimes searched for a way of extricating herself from a particular project even if this was guaranteed

173

to be successful. Pulling herself out of a hole, as she described it, would prove a tough uphill climb.

In January 1970, Sandie partnered "You Don't Have To Say You Love Me" Italian singer Pino Donaggio at San Remo. Critics regarded their song, "Che effeto me fa", as one of the better entries but it failed to make the final. The winners were Claudia Mori and Adriano Celentano. For five years after this, Sandie retreated into the shadows. In January 1977 she suffered a miscarriage and underwent an emergency operation which left her fighting for her life, then bedridden for weeks. Shortly after this harrowing experience, she became a Soka Gakkai Buddhist, introduced to the religion by a female friend who assured her that it would help her to cope with her marriage and financial problems. Jeff Banks had already converted to the modern Japanese faith, derived from Nicheren Buddhism and founded in 1975. The idea for induction came about after a night on the town.

"Spirits were involved—vodka," Sandie told the *Times*' Tim Teeman, "I woke up the next morning and asked her, if I started chanting, would it turn my life around?....My heart used to sink at the sound of the post. Was it more bills for Jeff? Was he going to jail? Was I? But then I'd chant and just send them all on to him."

Before her illness, Sandie had signed a short-term contract with CBS Records: this resulted in just two singles, both of which flopped. Pye for their part took advantage of her brief return to the limelight by putting out a compilation album, *The Sandie Shaw File*. Then on, for several years she appeared to be speeding swiftly downhill. There were the odd

174

cabaret dates overseas, and even a spell waitressing at Fatso's restaurant, in Soho. Sandie spoke openly about this in her memoirs and in radio interviews: the fact that she, who had never had a regular job before, managed to hold this one down for six weeks—often getting huge tips from the customers, including Andy Warhol—until the management asked her to leave because her celebrity presence, initially thought to have been a publicity stunt, was causing too much of a distraction. In 1982, eight months pregnant with his child, she married Nik Powell, with Richard Branson the co-founder of the Virgin Group. The religious ceremony took place at a Buddhist centre in Richmond, followed by a civil one four weeks later at Westminster Town Hall. Eve Taylor, though no longer Sandie's manager, was guest of honour—the last time they saw and spoke to each other. Not long afterwards, Taylor died suddenly: though no one knew her exact age she is thought to have been around seventy. "She was a remarkable, courageous woman, a woman full of love with nowhere for it to go," Sandie said of her. Few of the stars she had launched and nurtured attended her funeral—mostly because her estranged stepson, who inherited her fortune, never informed them of her death. Today she remains a forgotten figure, with not even a stone marking the spot in the London Jewish cemetery where she lies buried.

The following year, Nik Powell founded Palace Productions to shoot *Company Of Wolves*. Sandie was no stranger to acting: in the 1970s she played Ophelia in Glenda Jackson and husband Roy Hodges' (her Blackheath neighbours) London repertory production of *Hamlet*, and the title-role in

175

Shaw's *Saint Joan*—portraying Jeanne d'Arc as a sten-gun waving terrorist. Powell gave her cameo roles in two films. She played "Baby Boom's Mum" in the fantasy musical *Absolute Beginners* (1986) starring David Bowie and former call-girl Mandy Rice Davies—and "Edgeley's Girlfriend" in *Eat The Rich* (1987) with Bowie's wife, Angie. Interestingly, a few years later Nik Powell co-produced *Scandal*, centering around the Profumo scandal in which Davies had played a real-life central role. Powell also introduced Sandie to the BEF (British Electric Foundation) made up of various members of the Human League. The outfit invited her to record an "electronic" cover version of "Anyone Who Had A Heart" for their *Music Of Quality & Distinction* album, released on the Virgin label.

"It was a wholly new experience for me," she recalled. "Instead of singing with musicians I sang along to machines, no longer in a key or tempo but in a machine code number."

What most serious musicians would dismiss as a fake exercise included tracks by artistes as diverse as Tina Turner, Manfred Mann's Paul Jones, Billy Mackenzie—and television hostess Paula Yates. It brought Sandie—with Turner by the most talented person involved in the project—back into the public eye and saw Virgin putting the song out on a single. She also made her very first promotional video. The record narrowly missed the Top 50, and there was serious talk of Sandie recording a whole album or original material for Virgin. She also guested in The Pretenders' concert at London's Dominion Theatre, where she and Chrissie Hynde duetted on her old hit, "Girl Don't Come".

The Virgin album never materialised: instead, fourteen years after her last album Sandie wrote and recorded *Choose Life*, an initially private enterprise comprising 1,000 promotional copies, released in March 1983 in support of the Buddhist Choose Life World Peace Exposition which took place that spring in Kensington. Produced by Pete Bardens, the keyboards player with progressive rock band Camel, this contained oddities such as "Moontalk", "Dragon King's Daughter", and "The Mermaid". There was sufficient demand from fans to warrant the album being re-released on Nik Powell's Palace label, along with a single taken from it, "Wish I Was". This flopped, many believe because Sandie refused to emerge from her self-imposed exile to promote it, though she claimed that she had a legitimate excuse not to—she was pregnant with her second daughter, Amie. An unexpected surprise and triumph, however, was waiting just around the corner, courtesy of her most important professional meeting since the one with Adam Faith—with Morrissey and Johnny Marr of The Smiths.

Few would argue that Britain's most articulate singer-songwriter was a complex individual. He was a man who created his own culture, a personal world populated with foibles and unswaying opinion of just about every subject, not least of all in applying an almost fanatical religious fervour to his frequently offbeat likes and dislikes—obscure soap stars, literary figures, politicians, and the royal family. "Morrissey thinks God looks like James Dean and his wife looks like Joan Sims," Sandie later summed him up, adding that she had initially dismissed him as a crank.

The Smiths, formed in 1982, were one of the last truly great British rock bands whose songs covered hitherto taboo subjects, all sung by their handsome, willowy frontman in a haunting, melancholic voice. At the age of six, Morrissey had bought his first 45 rpm vinyl singles—amongst his favourites had been Marianne Faithfull's "Come And Stay With Me", and Sandie's "Always Something There To Remind Me". "I really, really did love these people," he told *Select*'s Mark Kemp in 1991, "I gave them my life, my youth. Beyond the perimeter of pop music there was a drop at the edge of the world." Throughout his teenage years, and in the wake of forming The Smiths with guitarist-songwriter Johnny Marr, Morrissey wrote copiously to his female idols: Dusty, Marianne, Twinkle and Cilla are thought to have received regular gushing missives from him, though so far as is known, Sandie was the only one to respond—and then only upon receipt of an "official correspondence" co-signed by Marr, and accompanied by a tape of their most recent composition, "I Don't Owe You Anything".

At this time, Sandie did not even know who The Smiths were, and once she *had* listened to them, though she defined Johnny Marr as the best guitarist she had *ever* heard—"But wasted on Morrissey!"— she was not particularly impressed with the then flat, almost tuneless Morrissey voice. She told Lucy O'Brien during a 2007 live interview for *Mojo*: "I felt that what was being asked of me was to be Morrissey's feminine side, but more overt. I could sing, and he can't really. He makes nice noises....and I knew how to find the tune in something, and how to put the melody out."

178

In his letter, Morrissey declared how he and Marr had written "I Don't Owe You Anything" especially for her, and that they were incurable Sandie Shaw fans who, having studied her material both day and night, felt that her future musical direction needed to avoid the "overt icky momism trap" which most of her Sixties contemporaries had fallen into. "The Sandie Shaw legend cannot be over yet," the missive concluded, "There is more to be done!"

To a certain extent, they were right. Sandie, like Dusty and Cilla had lapsed into a period where drossy material appeared to be the order of the day—certainly regarding her last three albums and her work with BEF. What she needed was a new, solidly-constructed, repertoire: lyrics with meaning, as opposed to the recent almost undecipherable third-rate tosh. In Morrissey's opinion, though this was untrue Sandie had recorded nothing worthwhile since "Heaven Knows I'm Missing Him Now" in 1969—their 1984 hit "Heaven Knows I'm Miserable Now" was based on this. Sandie's husband was a friend of Rough Trade's Geoff Travis, the label to which The Smiths were assigned, and it was he who orchestrated an introduction to the painfully shy singer, one which she said she had been initially reluctant to go through with because the tabloids had lambasted the group for their song, "Reel Around The Fountain", claiming that the subject was child molestation—it was actually about gay fellatio. "He didn't look like a child molester to me," Sandie observed in her memoirs, "As soon as he mobilised his mouth to speak, all my fears subsided. He was the perfect gentleman—a real little charmer—old-fashioned, even."

179

Early in 1984, Sandie temporarily replaced Morrissey as The Smiths' "singer" to perform a cover of the group's debut failed single, "Hand In Glove". This provided her with her first Top 30 hit in fifteen years and her last major hit to date. It must be observed that as with Dusty's collaboration late on in her career with the Pet Shop Boys, these records were bought mostly by fans of these pop outfits, and that they almost certainly would not have charted as solo efforts. Sandie appeared with The Smiths on *Top Of The Pops*—the gimmick being that while she dressed in black, wore stiletto heels and copied Morrissey's extraneous movements by writhing on the floor, the *musicians* appeared barefoot. A publicity shot of her and Morrissey depicted him at her feet, clutching a rosary.

Sandie also covered the song which had introduced her to the Smiths, "I Don't Owe You Anything", while Morrissey duetted with her on a never-released cover of "Girl Don't Come". There was also a lavishly orchestrated singalong version of "Please Help The Cause Against Loneliness", though arguably her best work with Morrissey was their duet of "Jeane". Like several of Sandie's early hits, this is a man's song—for whereas she strains to reach the top notes in "Hand In Glove" (her 1988 solo of this is comparatively poor), her delivery of "Jeane" is breathtakingly uncomplicated, and sends shivers down the spine.

Sandie's experience of working with Morrissey— along with her acceptance of her new faith— enabled her to take a fresh look at how she approached certain songs, particularly when it came to not wishing to change the gender.

"I was not imagining how someone else would feel," Sandie said. "I was doing something far more revolutionary than that. I was drawing not only from my present life, but from my multifarious past lifetimes as a woman, man, cat, tree, speck of dust or spark of light in the universe. I was attracted to each song because it was resonant of an aspect of first-hand experience."

Sandie and Morrissey are also known to have recorded "Sheila Take A Bow", The Smiths tribute to another icon, *A Taste Of Honey* playwright Shelagh Delaney. Like their duet of "Girl Don't Come", this has yet to surface.

Inasmuch as Morrissey had borrowed from Sandie so she would pay tribute to him by writing and recording "Steven (You Don't Eat Meat)"—her way also of displaying an obsession which was not that far removed from that of any other Smiths fan. The song was a gentle way of informing anyone who did not know already just how different Morrissey was: his vegetarianism and alleged celibacy, his preoccupation with his sickly constitution, his controlling nature, his fondness for flowers. "You dressed me in my gladrags, you in your gladioli," she sings. Later she would say how she had taken great trouble to impress him when turning up at his flat for the first time, only to be told, "I want you to walk in as if you've just walked in off the stage." Morrissey instructedd her how to dress, what jewellery to wear, and how to move in front of the camera. He (as a result of more correspondence) was a friend of Margi Clarke, one of the stars of *Letter To Brezhnev*, and arranged for Sandie to re-record "Always Something There To Remind Me", for the film's soundtrack. Similarly an aficionado of Lloyd Cole and punk poetess Patti Smith, he was behind Sandie's decision to record two songs by the former, including "Are You Ready To Be Heartbroken?" which with "Steven" on the B-side reached Number 68 in the charts—and Smith's "Frederick". She promoted the Cole song on the BBC's *Wogan*, in the same studio where she had taped her Song For Europe selections for *The Rolf Harris Show*. Fans who had not seen her in a while were amazed by her antics: wearing tight black denims and a floppy black coat, she performed the number she had described as "a million light years from the farting oompahs of 'Puppet On A String'", while twirling about the floor, finally flinging the coat over the cameraman's head before draping herself upside down on the on-set stairs!

There were other songs in honour of Morrissey and Marr, including "Go, Johnny, Go", and these augmented Sandie's repertoire when she embarked on her first tour in twenty years. Her performance at London's Town and Country Club was filmed, and commercially released. "It's a much more original approach to mid-life crisis than taking a toy boy lover," she said. I saw her at Wakefield Pussycat. The voice had changed but little over the years, but she had become flirtatious—descending to the auditorium to sit on men's laps, something the old Sandie would never have done. Some of Morrissey's eccentricity had rubbed off on her: like him, she had taken to rolling around on the stage. Again, an album was discussed. A previous one had been shelved by her falling pregnant again—her son, Jack, had been born in 1985.

A Rough Trade spokesman told me, "From the moment we began discussing the new album, Sandie was looking for an excuse to opt out. Such was her low self-esteem, she was convinced that it would flop. We believed otherwise, but she refused to listen."

Sandie also declined any idea (then) of re-recording her old hits, citing bad examples of trips down memory lane such as Lulu's "uninspired revamp" of "Shout", and Petula Clark's "pedestrian house version" of "Downtown". "I did not want my past turned into a seven-inch cliché," she said.

In 1988 Sandie had a change of heart about Rough Trade, and this resulted in *Hello Angel*—title courtesy of a postcard from Morrissey upon which he had scribbled in his almost illegible handwriting, "Hello angel, do you think I care too much?" Like many Smiths fans, Sandie is believed to have been devastated when, on account of their differences in character and temperament, Morrissey and Johnny Marr drew the curtain on their partnership.

"The Smiths was no ordinary group," she recalled. blaming Morrissey's problems on his insecurities. "They had something original, something special— they really touched people's lives."

Therefore who better to produce the album than 28-year-old Stephen Street, currently collaborating with Morrissey on his debut solo album, *Viva Hate*? "A lot of young people (older people too, come to think of it) are too awestruck to direct me properly, but I felt comfortable and secure with Stephen," she observes in her memoirs, a self-glorifying statement reminiscent of Joan Crawford's outburst in *Queen Bee*, when someone stares at her and she announces,

183

"Anybody would think he'd never *seen* a beautiful woman before!" Sandie's years in the wilderness, coupled with the British record-buying public's tendency to often forget and move on to someone else if their star has been absent for too long, had turned Sandie into one of those icons chosen by Morrissey for The Smiths' record sleeves—Yootha Joyce, Charles Hawtrey, Patricia Phoenix, etc—whom he had resurrected precisely *because* he had assumed the public had forgotten them. Effectively, Morrissey had taken this resurrection one step further because Sandie had responded to his call, otherwise she too might have found her past glory relegated to no more than a sleeve housing one of his kitchen sink drama compositions. Besides Stephen Street, Morrissey loaned her the drummer from *Viva Hate*, Andrew Paresi, and this spurred others into augmenting her cause: the Communards Richard Coles on keyboards, George Michael's bass-player Deon Estus, Chrissie Hynde on harmonica, and dee-jay Janice Long on castanets.

Afforded such talent, *Hello Angel* should have been a ground-breaking project. The Morrissey/Smiths influence is unmistakable, but compared with Sandie's previous albums, the content is grievously poor. Sorely lacking Eve Taylor's martinet influence and uncanny ability to find the right song at exactly the right time, Sandie had opted to write much of her own material—seven of the eleven songs were by her, four in collaboration with Chris Andrews who appeared to be losing his touch. As a singer, Sandie could never be faulted, but as a lyricist despite her best efforts for what she had in mind here, she was not in the same league as

184

Morrissey, whose theory had always been that the lyrics should take precedence over the music. With Sandie this does not work, resulting in a blandness beyond belief.

The album opens with "Nothing Less Than Brilliant", a so-so Smiths-style exercise in self-perception—the fact that no matter how many knocks one takes, one may still regard oneself as a precious stone. Morrissey fans have always insisted that the song was about him, Sandie's way of thanking him for the stupendous "Please Help The Cause Against Loneliness", arguably the only *great* song on the album and one which, acting on Morrissey's advice, Rough Trade put out as a single. Morrissey should have included this on *Viva Hate*, but instead gave it to Sandie. "Hello Angel", on the other hand, is barely decipherable. Of the other tracks "Strange Bedfellows" tells of gender-bending within marriage while "A Boy Called Johnny" was *not* a tribute to Johnny Marr, as was rumoured at the time, but a cover of a Waterboys song. "Comrade In Arms" is about Martinus, a young Dutch Buddhist who died of AIDS—Sandie was appointed his "buddy", and visited him at the hospice during the last weeks of his life. She finished writing it on the day he died, and recorded it in the middle of that same night.

The most unusual song on the album, and until recently the most mysterious, "Take Him" recounts an incident with Morrissey. *Viva Hate* was recorded at Wool Hall, near Bath, and Sandie was a frequent visitor to the studio where Morrissey made her welcome: "Offering hot flapjacks and cups of tea, he fussed around the old pine kitchen, like a broody hen." After one recording session, Morrissey, his entourage and Sandie headed for a local nightclub, entirely out of character for him, where they danced together. The idea for the song had come afterwards when Sandie had hugged him outside the studio. She recalled:

> Sinking into the softness of his red cashmere jumper. To my surprise he allowed himself to melt into his oneness....Although it was not quite goodbye, it certainly felt like adieu to the Morrissey I used to know.

"It was far less complicated than that," one of his musicians told me, some years later, "Sandie got close to Moz, and Moz got a hard-on. End of!"

The "red pullover" later cropped up in Morrissey's "Our Frank", which may explain why the alliance between he and Sandie ended so abruptly. The song, included in his 1991 *Kill Uncle* album, sees him berating someone over their "frank and open deep conversations", which only lead to him being disheartened, though their response is perhaps not what he was expecting: "Give it a rest....give me a drink and make it quick....or I'll be sick all over your red pullover!"

A few years down the line, Morrissey observed of his former idol, "I don't hear from her any more. It wasn't exactly a friendship made in heaven....let's just put it that way without saying any more."

The aforementioned musician offered a less complicated theory: "Sandie Shaw, through no fault of her own, got too close to him. And Moz never allows anyone to get too close, for fear of what they might find out."

More university tours followed, along with guest appearances at Gay Pride and AIDS charities events —a notable example of the latter took place at Wembley with The Communards, George Michael, and Boy George.

"The ultimate gay fantasy is to have a mother like me," Sandie told John Naughton of the *Observer*, "Straight men have a different kind of fantasy, which is nothing to do with me being their mother."

Later she told *Record Collector*'s Kit Levine, "I think the gay scene likes things to be larger than life. I love gay people. They like big divas, and I'm quite happy to play the role of the Big Dagenham Diva!"

At a Buddhist meeting, Sandie met Liverpool songstress and one time rival of Cilla Black, Beryl Marsden: the two became close friends and shared a house for a while with their various offspring. Then suddenly, though only in her mid-forties and still with much to offer, Sandie began retreating from the music scene. Her swansong of sorts was an appearance at the San Remo Festival in January 1990, when she partnered Milva with the song, "Sono felice". In retrospect, this was probably a mistake. Milva (born 1939), then as now Italy's biggest female singer, had participated in the contest twelve times, and this proved an unlucky thirteenth. Just as many had deemed Sandie too famous for Eurovision, so Milva was regarded by most fans as being above competing to prove how truly magnificent she was. She—not Sandie— brought the house down with their song, which failed to make the final round. The winning act was

187

called Pooh!—which just about said it all for a contest which had become decidedly old hat.

By this time, Sandie had begun working on her autobiography, *The World At My Feet,* which was published in 1991. Refusing to use a ghost-writer, she told her story with no chronology as such. The running commentary throughout the tome was her 1986 comeback tour, into which she incorporated flashbacks, flashbacks within flashbacks, and made a point of hardly mentioning her Sixties singles, preferring to focus on her marriages and family life, her traumas, highs and lows, and her rebirth by way of the Buddhist faith. Shortly after its publication, rather than heading back to the studio or the concert platform, she enrolled to study psychotherapy— firstly at Oxford, then at the University of London. She became a fully qualified practitioner in 1994.

At this time, Sandie released a compilation-retrospective album, *Nothing Less Than Brilliant.* What makes this of especially interest is the contrast in the material she had been singing back in the Sixties, now re-recorded, with some of the dross that had emerged two decades later.

"This album is the one I've always dreamed would be released," she told *Record Collector.* "It's like my complete world, a cross-generation family Christmas present, something for everyone."

Coinciding with the album's release was an interview with John Naughton of the *Observer,* whose subsequent feature was far more cynical than Sandie deserved, if not offensive in parts. She had lost none of her giggly wit and sparkle—she still hated "Puppet On A String", and more crucially she was still modestly aware of her importance to the British music scene, which Naughton had assigned to the past with a view to presenting her almost like some Sixties dinosaur—not that such an attitude was going to ruffle the feathers of *this* songbird, who proclaimed:

> If you are of iconoclastic proportions at all, people will readily enter into that transference of things with you. I think that's what being a star is all about, a massive kind of global transference back as to how well you actually work it. And, you know, reflecting is great! *I* see [the album] as the end of something, although the end of what, I'm not sure yet.

Effectively, the album heralded the closure of her singing career. Sandie Shaw had put her shoes back on, and they would stay on.

"If it came to the crunch, which career would you opt for—singing or psychology?" Kit Levine had asked her—bringing the response, "If I had to choose, I would have to move forward with my therapy work."

Soon afterwards, Sandie divorced Nik Powell and married for a third time. Tony Bedford was not from her show business side of the fence, but with him she achieved her most heartfelt ambition in recent years when they opened The Arts Clinic, a psychological health care centre in Harley Street. This specified not just in the treatment of troubled members of the arts world and the media, but the backstage people—the technicians and those unseen

189

faces essential to keep the industry ticking over.

In 2003, having won a legal battle to establish ownership of her back catalogue, Sandie licensed this worldwide to EMI: compilation albums were released in French, German, Spanish and Italian, and in Britain there was a fabulous 4-CD, 98-tracks box-set, *Nothing Comes Easy*. This contained the A and B-sides of all her British singles, plus several rare, previously unreleased tracks such as "Show Your Face", "Hurting You", and "Dear Madame". There was also a booklet featuring track-by-track commentary by Sandie herself.

In recent years Sandie has appeared spasmodically in radio interviews, always eager to talk about her past—even the darker days—with amazing candour, but she insists that there is no chance of her ever returning to the stage full-time aside from the occasional brief tour, as happened when she appeared on the circuit with pianist and presenter Jools Holland.

Currently Sandie likes to divide her time between England and France. She left Britain, she told Lucy O'Brien, because of Prime Minister Tony Blair and his Iraq-Afghanistan War policies. In the same interview, she explained *why* she would never affect a complete comeback, that she had no intention of following in Marianne's footsteps by singing Brecht and Weill, and further declared that she would never go on a crash diet or have a facelift—that, looking the way she did, she would never sell records!

It is a sad indication of today's celebrity climate: physical looks and whoever can screech loudest in television talent contests—Sandie called this new generation of female entertainers "show ponies"—

have replaced genuine talent. She *would* keep on recording new material, she concluded, but this would happen in her front room, and instead of record releases she would be posting these new songs on her website.

In 2001, *Life* magazine's Marina Cantacuzino had asked Sandie what the most pivotal moment of her life had been—clearly expecting some remarkable show business anecdote or revelation.

She had merely responded, "Every day is pivotal. Life is never dull and, if it is, I change it. I'm turning into Sandra Goodrich, the person I was!"

With Morrissey

In Shaw's *Saint Joan.*

With Nik Powell.

Sandie Shaw: 1960s Vinyl Discography

1964

As Long As You're Happy, Baby/ Ya-Ya-Da-Da
Pye 7N 15671

(There's) Always Something There To Remind Me/
Don't You Know
Pye 7N 15704

Girl Don't Come/ I'd Be Far Better Off Without You
Pye 7N 15743

(There's) Always Something There To Remind Me:
(There's) Always Something There To Remind Me;
Don't You Know; As Long As You're Happy, Baby;
Ya-Ya-Da-Da (EP) Pye NEP 24208

1965

I'll Stop At Nothing/ You Can't Blame Him
Pye 7N15783

Sandie: Everybody Loves A Lover; Gotta See My
Baby Every Day; Love Letters; Stop Feeling Sorry
For Yourself; Always; Don't Be That Way; It's In
His Kiss; Downtown; You Won't Forget Me;
Lemon Tree; Baby, I Need Your Loving; Talk
About Love. (Album) Pye NPL 18110

Long Live Love/ I've Heard About Him
Pye 7N 15841

Message Understood/ Don't You Count On It
Pye 7N 15940

Long Live Love: Long Live Love; You Can't Blame
Him; I'll Stop At Nothing; Girl Don't Come (EP)
Pye NEP 24220

How Can You Tell/ If Ever You Need Me
Pye 7N15987

Me: You Don't Love Me No More; I Don't Need
That Kind Of Lovin'; Down Dismal Ways; Oh No
He Don't (with Chris Andrews); When I Was A
Child; How Glad I Am; I Know; Till The Night
Begins To Die; Too Bad You Don't Want Me; One
Day; When I Fall In Love
(Album) Pye NPL 18122

Sandie: Talk About Love; Gotta See My Baby
Every Day; Don't Be That Way; Stop Feeling Sorry
For Yourself (EP) Pye NEP 24232

1966

Tomorrow/ Hurting You
Pye 7N 17036

Message Understood: Message Understood; How Can You Tell; If Ever You Need Me; Don't You Count On It (EP) Pye NEP 24236

Tomorrow: Tomorrow; I Know; When I Was A Child; Hurting You (EP) Pye NEP 24247

The Golden Hits of Sandie Shaw: (There's) Always Something There To Remind Me; Long Live Love; I've Heard About Him; I'd Be Far Better Off Without You; I'll Stop At Nothing; How Can You Tell; You Can't Blame Him; Don't You Count On It; Message Understood; If Ever You Need Me; Girl Don't Come (Album) Golden Guinea GGL 0360

Nothing Comes Easy/ Stop Before You Start
Pye 7N 17086

Nothing Comes Easy: Nothing Comes Easy; Stop Before You Start; Tomorrow; Hurting You (EP) Pye NEP 24254

Run/ Long Walk Home
Pye 7N 11763

Think Sometimes About Me/ Hide All Emotion
Pye 7N 17212

Run With Sandie Shaw: Run; Long Walk Home; Oh No Don't He; I Know (EP) Pye NEP 24264

1967

I Don't Need Anything/ Keep In Touch
Pye 7N 17239

Sandie Sings: Tomorrow; Talk About Love; Hurting You; Gotta See My Baby Every Day; Run; Stop Feeling Sorry For Yourself; Long Walk Home; Don't Be That Way; Stop Before You Start (Album) Golden Guinea GGL 0378

Sandie Shaw Chansons: Pourvu que ca dure; Toujours un coin qui me rappelle; Prends la vie du bon coté; Rien n'est fini; Ne compte pas sur moi; C'est toi qui le dit; Un tout petit pantin; Mais tu l'aimes; Tu las bien compris; Demain; Je ne marche pas; Ca glisse (Album) Vogue CMDPY 9654.

Puppet On A String/ Tell The Boys
Pye 7N 17272

Sandie Shaw In French: Mais tu l'aimes; Tu l'as bien compris; Pourvu que ca dure; Rien n'empechera l'amour (EP) Pye NEP 24271

196

Sandie Shaw In Italian: Viva l'amore con te; E ti avra; Domani; Quello che tu cerci amica (EP) Pye NEP 24273

Puppet On A String: Puppet On A String; Think Sometimes About Me; I Don't Think You Want Me Anymore; Keep In Touch; Stop Before You Start; Hide All Emotion; Tell The Boys; Don't You Count On It; No Moon; Long Walk Home; I'd Be Far Better Off Without You; Had A Dream Last Night (Album) Pye SPL 18182

Tell The Boys: Tell The Boys; I'll Cry Myself To Sleep; Had A Dream Last Night; Ask Any Woman (EP) Pye NEP 24281

Tonight In Tokyo/ You've Been Seeing Her Again Pye 7N 17346

You've Not Changed/ Make Me Cry Pye 7N 17378

Love Me, Please Love Me: Love Me, Please Love Me; One Note Samba; Smile; Yes, My Darling Daughter; Ne me quitte pas; Every Time We Say Goodbye; The Way That I Remember Him; Hold 'im Down; I Get A Kick Out Of You; Time After Time; That's Why; By Myself (Album) Pye SPL 18205

1968
Today/ London
Pye 7N 17441

Don't Run Away/ Stop
Pye 7N 17504

Show Me/ One More Lie
Pye 7N 17564

Together/ Turn On The Sunshine
Pye 7N 17587

Those Were The Days/ Make It Go
Pye 7N 17611

The Sandie Shaw Supplement: Route 66; Homeward Bound; Scarborough Fair; Right To Cry; The Same Things; Our Song Of Love; (I Can't Get No) Satisfaction; Words; Remember Me; Change Of Heart; Aranjuez Mon Amour; What Now My Love (Album) Marble Arch MAL 1164

Reviewing The Situation: Reviewing The Situation; Lay Lady Lay; Mama Roux; Sun In My Eyes; Walking The Dog; Oh Gosh; Your Time Is Gonna Come; Coconut Grove; Sympathy For The Devil (Album) Pye SPL 18323

1969
Monsieur Dupont/ Voice In The Crowd
Pye 7N 17675

Think It All Over/ Send Me A Letter
Pye 7N 17726

Heaven Knows I'm Missing Him Now/ So Many Things To Do
Pye 7N 17821

1970 (recorded 1969)
By Tomorrow/ Maple Village
Pye 7N 17894

Lulu

She was the wee Scots lassie with the voice which could demolish a skyscraper. Where the other Brit Girls made their mark on the pop scene with one song in particular, Lulu did it with a single line: "Weeeeeeeeel, you make me wanna shout!"

Hers was a bigger struggle than most, from a poverty-stricken Glasgow tenement block to superstardom and wealth, and by way of more chart misses than hits—though she managed to combine the two by having the distinction of having one single top the US *Billboard* Hot 100 without it having even entered the UK charts.

Lulu excelled with R & B and raucous rock, but never quite managed the knack of putting over a ballad like her contemporaries. She starred in one good movie, married and divorced a Bee Gee, won Eurovision and saw a slump in her career. Then, following in the footsteps of Dusty and Sandie, she briefly returned to chart glory, singing with a boy band. Today she divides her time between television appearances, the odd tour, fashion promotion, and her family.

1: Take Me As I Am!

She was born Marie McDonald McLaughlin Lawrie on 3 November 1948, at Glasgow's Lennox Castle Hospital. Home for the Lawries was at 55 Soho Street, in the city's tough Lennoxtown suburb, parts of which were then little more than a slum. Her father, Eddie, worked as an offal dresser in Glasgow Meat Market. Her mother, Betty, appears to have been ever the long-suffering housewife. She and Eddie had married in 1947, and for years Betty would put up with his hard-drinking and ferocious tempers. In her memoirs, *I Don't Want To Fight*, Lulu recalls her father arriving home from the pub, bladdered, and beating his wife black and blue. "Some people would rather be beaten and abused than ignored, particularly when they were lonely and hurting," she observes, almost excusing him for what was accepted then as normal behaviour for many hard-up Northern couples. And next morning when he had sobered up, like many wife-bashers, Eddie would be wracked with guilt upon surveying the damage he had caused, not just to Betty but to their tiny flat, one of nine in a tawdry tenement block with no hot water and shared toilet facilities. And yet, when not drunk and rowing with his wife, who apparently could "eff and blind" with the best of them *and* hit him back, Eddie could be unbelievably tender and generous.

At five, Marie was enrolled at Campbellfield Street Infants School, though she had barely settled in here when she was uprooted to Thompson Street Priory when the Lawries moved to a larger flat. Still without hot water, this was on Garfield Street, but a stone's throw from their old address. "There weren't so many poorly dressed kids and runny noses," she recalled of the only slightly better neighbourhood where rival gangs roamed the streets day and night, few of whose members ventured outside unless "tooled up". One friend, she remembered, often walked around armed with an iron bar or an axe! The early pages of her memoirs tell of slashings, thugs bottling each another, beatings, kickings and obligatory foul language. "In Glasgow," she writes, "You didn't turn the other cheek, unless you wanted that one sliced open as well."

Hard as nails they may have been, but by all accounts the Lawries were not as poor as their struggling neighbours assumed. Eddie stole large amounts of meat from the market where he worked, sold it cheap to local butchers and earned more from this than he did his regular job. Some of the extra money went on drink, some Betty filched from his pockets while he was sleeping off his excesses, but most of it was spent on treating his family—clothes, weekend outings they would never have afforded otherwise to the Isle of Bute where the Lawries rented a holiday apartment, visits to the theatre and cinema, and records which were played on their radiogram, the only one in their block.

Like many of her generation, Marie's childhood musical influences tended to reflect those of her parents: Perry Como, Mario Lanza, Teresa Brewer, Kay Starr. She cites her first public performance as 2 June 1953—the evening of Queen Elizabeth's coronation—an event for which most working class British families purchased their first television set. *The* song marking the occasion was "In A Golden Coach", a big hit for the Billy Cotton Band—Marie sang this during her street's party celebrations, earning herself the nickname "*the rerr wee chanter*" from her father. Then on she sang regularly at family get-togethers, until a trip to Blackpool later that summer got her hooked on talent contests. The first of these saw her performing Kay Starr's "The Wheel Of Fortune", wearing a hoop-dress and emulating the American star's on-stage gyrations, and walking off with the first prize of 50 shillings.

Upon the family's return to Glasgow, now that the show business bug had bit, Marie began singing and reciting poetry in Robert Burns competitions. By now, her "coalman's voice" had been brought to the attention of local bandleader Billy McPhee, who fronted the 30-piece Caledonian Accordion Band, based at the Orange Lodge, in Bridgton. She was eight years old when McPhee hired her on a weekly fee of 30 shillings as part-time vocalist: singing The Platters' "The Great Pretender", she made her professional debut during a Sunday evening concert for members of the Lodge. At around the same time she cut her first "disc" in a record store booth—Frankie Vaughan's "The Garden Of Eden", coupled with "All Of Me". This would resurface many years later, when Eamonn Andrews "collared" her for *This Is Your Life*.

Over the next three years, Marie sang regularly with the Caledonian Accordion Band, mostly the latest Transatlantic hits by Connie Francis and Neil Sedaka. She handed her earnings over to her mother, ostensibly to help support her increasing family: the Lawrie's first son, Billy, had come along in 1952 and in September 1958, Betty gave birth to a second daughter, Edwina. Betty only ploughed the money back into Marie's act, buying the finest materials and making her stage clothes, and taking her to one of the most expensive hairdressers in Glasgow. Marie repaid her by doing the housework and helping out with the children after school.

School, once Marie had experienced a taste of the spotlight, became an avoidable chore. Her dream, she said, was to work as a hairdresser and sing with a band on weekends—eventually she aspired to get married, have lots of children, and live in a better part of town, in a nice house with its own facilities. No more shared toilets! Meanwhile, whenever she could she wagged a day off school, but only to help around the house while Betty looked after the new baby. "Caring for a baby was much more attractive than algebra and logarithms," she recalled.

Marie developed into something of a tomboy, and despite her diminutive size—fully grown, she would only measure 5 feet 1 inch—proved handy with her fists if anyone picked on her or Billy, no matter how big they were. Eddie Lawrie had drilled into her his own philosophy for dealing with troublemakers: "Hit them wi' everythin' yer've got and make sure they don't get up. If they do, run like fuck—it means they're tougher than you!"

Marie sang with Billy McPhee's Accordion Band until poached from him by a Mr. Adamson, who managed the Bellrocks, a local four-piece outfit, average age seventeen. Adamson's son, Billy, was their drummer. Within weeks of joining them she was working regularly at Barrowlands, one of the city's top venues. The group also travelled farther afield, touring US airbases, resulting in the Lawries relaxing the 10.30 pm curfew that had been imposed on their daughter until now—hardly surprising considering some of the characters roaming around their neighbourhood after dark.

Marie's repertoire, which suited the Bellrocks' style perfectly, now included songs by Brenda Lee and Ray Charles. She was still at school and hating it, but the envy of her classmates because she was starting to make a name for herself on the music circuit. At eleven she moved from Thompson Street Primary to Whitehill Secondary, where she got into bother with the headmistress for dying her mousey-coloured hair carrot-red. This caused such a fuss that her parents, rather than admonish her as advised to do so by her teachers, transferred her to Onslow Secondary, just down the road. At around this time she met up with another local band, The Gleneagles, so-named after the famous golf course, who played Sunday evenings at the Lindella Ballroom, in Glasgow's city centre—when not working with The Bellrocks, Marie sang with them to a much more appreciative crowd.

The Gleneagles line-up comprised vocalist and guitarist Jimmy Dewar (who later joined Stone The Crows and became something of a minor rock legend), lead guitarist Rock Nelson, bassist Tommy Tierney, drummer Dave Nelson, and saxophonist Jimmy Smith. Because they dressed smarter than the Bellrocks—tartan jackets, button-down shirts and neatly-pressed trousers—they pulled in a more upmarket crowd, more so once Marie joined them, never settling for less than centre-stage and with her foghorn voice more than capable of making herself heard above the noisiest crowd. Their repertoire was much more extensive than that of the Bellrocks, and incorporated recent hits by Ike and Tina Turner, Lee Dorsey, and other black American stars. Not long afterwards they recruited an extra singer: Alec Bell, three years Marie's senior, became her first serious boyfriend.

A big act in Scotland at the time was Alex Harvey (1935-82), whose popularity had soared since performing in Hamburg with The Beatles and some of the big Merseyside groups. When Harvey returned to Glasgow at the end of 1962, Marie and the Gleneagles went to see him. It was widely anticipated that the perpetually leather-clad Harvey and his band would be rivals of the Fab Four— something which would never happen. For Marie, the revelation came with his opening number. "Shout Parts 1 & 2" had been written and recorded by the Isley Brothers in 1959, and though not a big hit—it had reached Number 47 on the *Billboard* chart—it had sold steadily over the years and earned them a gold record. That same year in Australia, rocker Johnny O'Keefe had taken his version to Number 3, and in 1962 Joey Dee & The Starfighters had taken it to Number 6 in America. Marie picked up the tune after a single hearing, which was not difficult bearing in mind its repetitive simplicity. The Gleneagles spent the next day rehearsing it, and that same evening added it to their set.

The Gleaneagles' big break occurred when they were heard by David Bell, who produced the children's magazine *Round-Up* for a Scottish television station. Bell did not however hire the group—just Marie, who in a local take-off of the BBC's *Juke Box Jury* was invited to participate as one of the judges in the programme's record review section. Another panellist was John Reid: during the next decade he would manage Elton John, and Queen. Marie's bubbly personality, which exploded from the small screen was sufficient to see a number of entrepreneurs trying to woo her away from the group. One was Richard Stern, a wealthy local businessman who offered to manage her, in partnership with the Lindella's Alec Houston. Another was Stern's friend, Tony Gordon, visiting Glasgow in search of premises to open a French-style discotheque, a craze starting on this side of the Channel. He subsequently opened Le Phonograph with his brother-in-law, Gerry Massey.

It was Tony Gordon who hit on the idea of finding Marie a record deal, though first he decided that she would have to become more nationally (i.e. in Scotland) known. He enlisted the help of another Gordon—Gordon Reed penned the show business column for the *Scottish Daily Express*, which had recently launched a campaign to recruit artistes for a Scottish pop invasion which the paper hoped would rival the one currently taking place in Liverpool. The bid to secure a contract failed despite numerous auditions with visiting record company executives.

Scotland's music scene was currently monopolised by middle-of-the-road acts such as Moira Anderson, Kenneth McKellar, the Billy Cotton Band Show's Kathie Kay, and in the pop world by skiffle star Lonnie Donegan and "Freight Train" singer Nancy Whiskey. Soon there would be just one exception, a diminutive teenager named Marie Lawrie. The representative from EMI was so impressed with her rendition of The Platters' "Only You" that he informed Tony Gordon that the contract was hers, if she wanted it. Naturally, as she was only fourteen the matter had to be discussed with her parents. They agreed, and in October 1963 she was invited to audition at the Columbia Studios, in Hampstead.

Marie had never been to London. England in those days, she said, was a foreign country to most Glaswegians. Tony Gordon, Alec Houston, and the Gleneagles all travelled with her. She chose two songs for her audition: "Shout", naturally, and Gene Pitney's "Twenty Four Hours From Tulsa", to prove that she could also sing ballads. She failed the audition—EMI claimed she was not quite what they were looking for, but they did put in a good word with Decca, who had famously rejected the Beatles and signed the Rolling Stones. Many years later, when the company released *Shout! The Complete Decca Recordings*, John Reed observed in the CD notes, "If the Beatles had an equivalent in terms of girl vocalists in Dusty, then the Rolling Stones should have looked no further than Decca labelmate Lulu."

The record company took Marie on board, though several "niggles" had to be ironed out before a contract could be signed. Her two years with the label would prove exceedingly difficult at times. Firstly, Decca wanted nothing to do with Richard Stern or Alec Houston, while Gordon Reed felt that *he* should have some say in managing her— claiming that he had effectively discovered her and brought her to Decca's attention in the first place. Marie wanted to be handled exclusively by Tony Gordon, but he had enough on his plate with the recently opened Le Phonograph, and was currently negotiating opening a similar venue in Manchester.

208

He did however agree to act as intermediary with Decca until she appointed someone else. Next, Decca asked Marie to ditch the Gleneagles: if she was going to record for the company, they said, she would be assigned session musicians. On this issue she stood her ground: no Gleneagles, no Marie Lawrie. Decca capitulated, and after signing the contract, Marie and the group returned to Glasgow, where she eagerly awaited her fifteenth birthday so that she could leave school. In the meantime, Tony Gordon found her the perfect "manager"—his sister, former mezzo-soprano Marian Massey.

When Marian Massey met Marie and the Gleneagles early in 1964 she was a housewife living with her entrepreneur husband, Gerry, in a large Victorian house in Holland Park—a far cry from what Marie was used to. The youngster had caught a cold during the journey from Scotland, and recalls how Massey fussed over her:

> I looked awful. My hair was in rollers under a fur beret and I wore a baggy cardigan to keep warm. She swanned through the door wearing a three-quarter-length, anthracite-grey Persian lamb coat, with a huge chinchilla collar, a pencil-straight skirt and high-heel Chanel court shoes. She looked every inch a film star and was unquestionably the most glamorous creature I had ever laid eyes on in real life.

Despite her lack of experience, Massey would prove a shrewd but kindly, no nonsense businesswoman without whom Marie Lawrie almost certainly would never made it to the top. The first stop was the studio, where "Shout" and its B-side, "Forget Me Baby", were completed in three takes—after which the lady with the "rounded vowels and clipped consonants" whisked her roughly-spoken charge off to a pharmacy, then back to her home where she pampered her until she had recovered from her cold.

One week later, Marian Massey flew to Glasgow to meet the Lawries. This must have been a culture shock for both parties, though they appear to have got along well. Massey confessed that she did not know the slightest thing about managing a pop star, but that she would learn as she went along. If this was true, she learned fast. Her first important decision was a change of monicker—her protegéé would never get anywhere, she declared, with a tongue-twister of a name like Marie McDonald McLaughlin Lawrie! The singer recalled how she and Tony Gordon were sitting at the piano in the Masseys' living room when Marian, ponderously pacing up and down, suddenly exclaimed, "Well, all I know is that she's a real *lulu* of a kid!"

She had been baptised for life and in December 1963 shortly after her fifteenth birthday, Marie/Lulu left school. Two weeks earlier, the Lawries had received yet another visit from the school inspector, when Betty is said to have made her much-repeated quote, "Do ye nae read the papers or watch tv? She's a pop star, now!" True or not, it makes for a great anecdote. In leaving school, Marie was also saying goodbye to her childhood, though by relocating to London, essential for her career, she was concerned about her parents' welfare. Betty was pregnant again —soon afterwards she gave birth to her second son,

Gordon—and she was afraid that if she left her mother and father to fight unsupervised, one might inflict serious harm on the other.

To handle Lulu's publicity Decca hired Les Perrin, formerly a press officer for the Rolling Stones—a hard-drinking, chain-smoking, aggressive individual known to have moved mountains to prevent unsavoury stories about some of his protégés hitting the headlines. Perrin organised a press-launch at an exclusive Italian restaurant in Fleet Street—and no sooner had Lulu arrived than she was made to give an impromptu performance of "Shout", standing on a chair so that everyone could see her. The next morning the papers—even the fussier broadsheets—published pictures of the event with some variation of the caption, "New Girl Lulu Makes You Wanna Shout!" As had happened with Dusty Springfield, some journalists who had been sent demo discs without photographs had assumed they would be seeing a black singer, which Lulu considered the greatest compliment of all.

"Shout" was released to critical acclaim on 15 April 1964, with the names Lulu & The Luvvers (the former Gleneagles) on the label. "Weeeeeeeel, you know you wanna make me shout," she bawls, a capella, in what was arguably the most raucous introduction to any Sixties song. As the title suggests, she shouts and strains all the way through, effecting little in the way of a tune—yet it is GOOD, far better than anything that any American rock singer came up with at the time. Today, no one cares who introduced the song, or who may have covered it since 1964. The song *belongs* to Lulu, and will be forever associated *only* with her. On the

211

flipside was the equally noisy "Forget Me Baby",
penned by Alex Houston and Tony Gordon. The
single was released at exactly the right time to
coincide with the Beatles-Merseyside-Brit Girls
phenomenon—had Lulu been launched any earlier,
she might have ended up travelling the same short
commercial road as Helen Shapiro. *Melody Maker*
hailed her "The Raving Rocker"—at the end of the
year the magazine's readers voted her their Brightest
British Hope.

The song was played to death on the radio, and
promoted on all the regular television shows,
beginning with *Ready, Steady, Go!*, where Lulu met
John Lennon and Paul McCartney for the first time.
The single shot to Number 7 in the charts, and
remained in the Top 30 for three months. Lulu was
feted everywhere she went, yet admitted to crying
herself to sleep most nights because she was
missing her family. A large portion of her earnings
was spent on phone calls to her mother, who
suffered from depression after she left home.

"Who would iron their clothes and polish their
shoes?" Lulu asked herself, "Who would keep them
safe when Mum and Dad were fighting?"

Initially, Lulu tried to get home most weekends,
but as her workload increased, this became virtually
impossible. Her parents were comfortable with the
fact that she was safe. After spending a few weeks
in hotels or guest-houses, the musicians moved into
a flat, and Lulu moved in with Marian Massey's
parents, who lived in St John's Wood. Here, she was
given her own self-contained apartment—the first
time, digs aside, that she had not had to share a
room with someone else. To put the Lawries' minds

at rest, Massey flew the whole family down to London to see for themselves how respectable her new life as a pop star was. Even so, Betty Lawrie would never like Massey or forgive her for taking her daughter away from her—indeed, Lulu claimed that she even contacted one Scottish newspaper with the story that Massey had *kidnapped* her, but that Les Perrin had stopped this getting printed! Perrin also intervened when, during one argument too many with Eddie, Betty took a tumble and ended up in the local hospital suffering from concussion. This time, the neighbours threatened to contact the press: Perrin reached for his cheque book once more, and another scandal was averted.

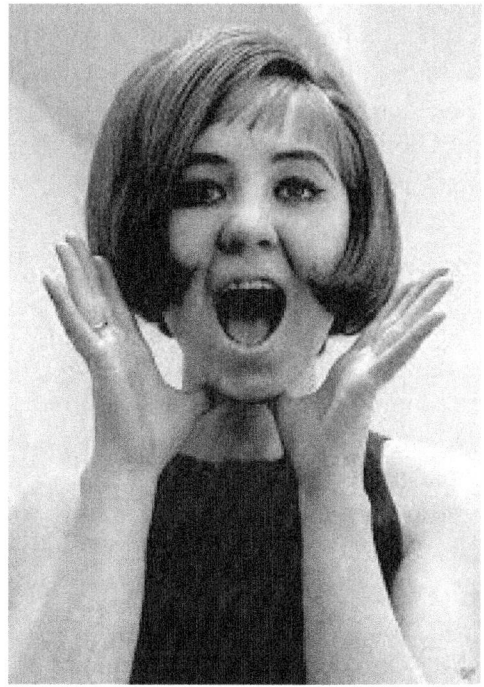

Shout"

2: What A Wonderful Feeling!

Though not a control freak in the style of Eve Taylor, Marian Massey did have a job on her hands with Lulu—not in controlling her behaviour, for in this respect she appears to have been a model teenager, but in teaching her how not to dress like a tomboy, and in ridding her of the rougher edge of her frequently undecipherable Glaswegian accent. She also had Lulu's teeth fixed, after watching her on *Juke Box Jury*—one of her gold fillings showed up black when filmed in monochrome. Otherwise, she stayed exactly the same as when Massey had first seen her. Neither was it obligatory to assign her a weekly allowance, like some of the other under-age Brit Girls: living on a rough-and-ready council estate had taught her how be prudent with money.

Lulu's first gala performance as a professional entertainer took place in Glasgow in June 1964. *The Big Beat Show* should have seen her billed below Dave Berry & The Cruisers. Such a fuss was made over the fact that she was going home that the venue manager demanded she be given top billing. Lulu and Sheffield-born Berry—about to release his hit, "The Crying Game"—caused less of a commotion than the band booked to open the show. The High Numbers comprised Roger Daltrey, John Entwistle, Pete Townshend and Keith Moon who had started off the year as The Who, and would revert to their more famous monicker after this summer tour. Lulu was so taken up with the group—and the ill-fated Moon by her—that she invited them back to her parents' flat for supper after the show, a real eye-opener for a neighbourhood just getting used to having one star in their midst.

On 12 July, Lulu moved further up the musical ladder when supporting the Rolling Stones at the Queen's Hall, Leeds. Here, their manager Andrew Loog Oldham decided that Mick Jagger and Keith Richard—having penned "As Tears Go By" for Marianne—would write a song for Lulu. They came up with "Surprise, Surprise" (nothing to do with the Cilla song of the same title) which they claimed would prove the ideal companion piece to "Shout". A zippy, honky-tonk hard rock number, it might have achieved the same success had Decca not relegated it to a B-side.

The successor to "Shout", released in August, was the clap-along "I Can't Hear You No More", a Gerry Goffin-Carol King hit for Betty Everett also covered by Dusty Springfield. Despite some nifty session work from future Led Zepellin guitarist Jimmy Page and Lulu's tremendous performance—the B-side, Jerry Novac's Chiffons-style "I Am In Love" was almost as good—the single flopped.

Lulu loved working with Page, and later observed, "We thought the little farting sound from his guitar was unbelievable, way out there in the stratosphere as a new sound. *Everyone* was thrilled about that!"

Neither was it third time lucky with Lulu's polished interpretation of "Here Comes The Night", released in November. An original composition by R & B songwriter Bert Berns (who had recently founded Shout Records, no connection to Lulu) it was without any doubt her finest recording during her first year with Decca, but stalled at Number 50 in the charts. The following year, the band Them narrowly missed the UK top slot with what many considered an inferior version of the song—pushing

215

their Irish-born frontman, Van Morrison, on the road towards international fame. Bronx-born Berns (1929-67)—a pioneer of early rock, soul and mambo—had given the Beatles "Twist And Shout". Dusty had covered his "Take Another Piece Of My Heart", and Berns would famously produce Wilson Pickett, Solomon Burke, The Drifters, along with this and several other early tracks for Lulu. The single's failure and that of Lulu's first release of 1965—Carol King's "Satisfied", c/w "Surprise, Surprise"—gave Decca serious misgivings about having taken on the young Scottish singer, who at this stage in her career seemed set to be relegated to the one-hit wonder category which included such otherwise talented individuals as Susan Maughan.

Because her singles were selling poorly at a time when record companies released EPs containing chart hits and their B-sides, Decca released just one of these in the UK—*Lulu* sold more copies than any single since "Shout" and did not contain *any* previously released material. Holland-Dozier-Holland's "(Love Is Like A) Heatwave" had been a recent US hit for Martha & The Vandellas—the first Motown song to be Grammy-nominated. Smokey Robinson's "What's Easy For Two Is So Hard For One" had given Mary Wells & The Andantes a minor success—the "two" in the title refers to the couple who are in love, the "one" the preacher who the narrator hopes will marry them. "Nothing Left To Do But Cry" was an early number penned by Bread's David Gates. Jack Keller and Gerry Goffin's "The Trouble With Boys", the best of the four tracks here, had been a hit for Little Eva.

In May 1965, Lulu & The Luvvers participated in

the Brighton Song Festival and were runners up with Les Reed and Robin Conrad's "Leave A Little Love". The other contestants included Dave Berry, Cliff Bennett & The Rebel Rousers, Maureen Evans, Helen Shapiro, Billy Fury—and Marianne Faithfull, who's "Go Away From My World", by far the best song in the contest, was pipped to the post by Kenny Lynch's now forgotten winning entry, "I'll Stay By You". Indeed, there was talk at the time that the voting may have been rigged. Lulu certainly thought so. Decca had been toying with releasing "He Don't Want Your Love Anymore", the English adaptation of "Vous pouvez me dire"—a smash hit in France for former deejay Annie Philippe. This far superior song now ended up on the flipside of "Leave A Little Love", which nevertheless reached Number 8 in the charts.

In the meantime, as with many pop acts of the day Lulu was rushed into a hurriedly cobbled together feature film—and what a mess this turned out to be! Like most of the genre salvaged only by its music, today it is regarded as little more than a curiosity. *Gonks Go Beat* (gonks were small furry animal toys, very much in fashion at the time, and the theme tied in with the latest beat craze) was written and directed by Robert Hartford-Davis, who devised the tagline, "The Craziest Musical Adventure Ever On Planet Earth". It certainly lived up to his boast. A modern take on *Romeo & Juliet*/*West Side Story* with lots of Lambrettas and cheesy hairstyles, it told of the musical rivalry between the inhabitants of two islands, Beatland and Balladisle, who clash annually for the Golden Guitar, and first prize of a trip around the world. Sent down to earth to bring a boy and girl from the opposing camps together in unholy matrimony is alien Kenneth O'Connor— adding to the mayhem are character actors Arthur Mullard, Frank Thornton, and later *Casualty* regular Derek Thompson. Drummer Ginger Baker and The Graham Bond Organisation are the only ones worth watching in the musical segments. Lulu & The Luvvers had two numbers by Mike Leander: "The Only One" is an instantly forgettable pop ballad, while "Choc Ice" is one of the most excruciating songs ever performed by a Brit Girl. Lulu screams it from start to finish. Thankfully where her celluloid career was concerned there would be better things to come.

The unexpected success of "Leave A Little Love" had restored Lulu's confidence, and Decca's: until this point, they had been about to shelve plans for her recording her debut album. This was assembled even more hurriedly than the film, and released as "Something To Shout About"—unusually, there were sixteen tracks instead of the regulation twelve. The album should have contained the usual Brit Girls fare for the time—American R & B standards, Motown covers, the odd spruced up standard. On account of the rush to get it into the shops for Lulu's autumn tour, another rushed exercise, Decca threw in a sizeable quota of tack, such as the *Gonks Go Beat* songs and her recent failed singles and their B-sides. It did not match up to Marianne's and Dusty's debut albums by some way: even so, the fans liked it enough for it to peak at Number 7 in the charts. Also, what little new material it contained was far better than the songs Decca was putting out on singles.

218

Side One opens with "You Touch Me Baby", a "doop-doop" ditty from the repertoire of obscure US quartet Baby Jane & The Rockabyes spawned in the wake of the Joan Crawford-Bette Davis *schlockfest* movie, "What Ever Happened To Baby Jane?" "Like a beam from an X-ray machine, you see right through me," Lulu expostulates in this quick-fire repartee which *might* have seen her with a hit on her hands, had Decca put it out as a single. The same may be said of Mike Stoller's "You'll Never Leave Her", whose guitar riffs bear more than a passing resemblance to The Seekers' "I'll Never Find Another You". Introduced by soul singer Freddie Scott, with its South of the Border feel and tricky key-changes it is not the kind of number one would usually associate with Lulu, whose voice was never quite as malleable as that of Sandie Shaw, who she gives every impression of emulating here.

"I'll Come Running Over" was another song from the pen of Bert Berns. Liverpool-born Lynn Randell had a hit with it in Australia. It is not in the same class as his earlier "Here Comes The Night"—there is far too much repetition of the title, which Lulu annoyingly drawls, "I'll come running *ooover*!" "She Will Break Your Heart", originally recorded by Chicago-based gospel outfit Curtis Mayfield & The Impressions, is on the other hand sensational. Lulu's beautiful, tempered performance is almost in the fashion of a Dinah Washington-Brook Benton duet, and may well be definitive. Again, this should have been released as a single—by not doing so, it was as if Decca *wanted* Lulu to be a failure. Not so good is her take on Holland-Dozier-Holland's "Can I Get A Witness", recently a hit for Marvin Gaye—

219

again, she drawls out the title-line, raucously emphasising the word "witness". Dusty had covered it much better.

Side Two of the album has a tremendous version of Roosevelt Sykes and Leon Carr's 1937 blues classic, "Night Time Is The Right Time", recorded by Sykes two years after his partner's early death. "So In Love" is *not* the Cole Porter standard from *Kiss Me Kate*, as stated in some album credits, but a cover of The Tymes' US Number One of 1963. A fine reading it is too, more polished and engaging than the later cover by Eagles singer Timothy B Schmit, and the cheesy version by Tony Orlando & Dawn. "Dream Lover" is dreadful, almost as bad as the *Gonks Go Beat* songs. Bobby Darin, had topped the UK charts with this in 1959: Lulu sings it way too fast, shrieking so much that one is glad when it is all over. Thankfully, Decca changed their minds about releasing it as a single, though it would be a case of history repeating itself with the August and October follow-ups to "Leave A Little Love"—"Try To Understand" (c/w Not In The Whole World) and "Tell Me Like It Is" (c/w Stop Fooling Around). Three of the four songs were taken from the album, at a time when this rarely happened. The former stalled at Number 25 in the charts, while the second single flopped.

At around this time, Lulu & The Luvvers recorded a track for *14 Great Artistes: Lord Taverner's Charity Album*. "Just One Look" later provided The Hollies with a massive hit. For twenty years, until being re-released on a budget compilation album, it would remain one of Lulu's most sought after songs. Other stars performing similarly exclusive songs on the album included Kathy Kirby, The Bachelors, Tom Jones, Dave Berry, Billy Fury—and the Rolling Stones, whose contribution was "Surprise, Surprise", the number they had written for Lulu.

In the meantime, "Leave A Little Love" had proved a hit in Germany, resulting in Lulu releasing her first foreign language single. Written by Christian Bruhn (whose "Monsier Dupont" gave Sandie a hit), "Wenn du da bist" c/w "So fing es an" was however no great shakes, and bombed. Following a lightning trip to Germany to promote it, in January 1966 she and The Luvvers flew to Poland—where the Hollies were in the middle of a 12-day tour. As such, Lulu was the first British female singer to perform behind the Iron Curtain. It was, she recalled, an unpleasant experience and the concerts, though well-attended, proved an ordeal.

"It looked like the end of the world. Out of every [train] window I seemed to see crumbling cities, blackened by soot and haunted by the legacy of war," Lulu recalled.

"If anyone stood up to give you a standing ovation the military police waded in with batons," observed Marlene Dietrich, who followed her around on the tour circuit.

Thus "unruly" fans expressing their appreciation by approaching the stage, waving autograph books, were dragged outside and beaten. If the acts sang anything extant of their set-list, this was deemed as "appropriation of propaganda" and resulted in the manager switching off the power, plunging the place into darkness.

Upon her return to Britain, Lulu toured with the Beach Boys, and filmed a television commercial for

Lux soap—setting a precedent for later in her career when her name would be used to promote make-up, clothes, and her own brand of hairspray. There was a parting of the ways with The Luvvers—Decca had never wanted them in the first place, and most of the new tracks on *Something To Shout About* had been recorded with session musicians leaving Lulu's band feeling disgruntled. Maybe *they* were also a little disappointed in the way things had turned out with her. In the beginning, she had been one of the boys: The Luvvers and the frontwoman *they* had adopted and who had enjoyed equal importance in their line-up, only to have her increasing popularity see pushed them more and more into the background. Lulu pleaded with the Decca executives to keep them on but they refused to listen. Splitting from the Luvers put paid to her relationship with Alec Bell.

"If we had stayed in Scotland, we probably would have married by the time I was seventeen," she reflected.

The move saw Lulu turning solo. Until now she had been listed on the Decca roster as part of a group, Lulu & The Luvvers, the name which appeared on record labels. Though not as commercially successful as Cilla, Dusty, Marianne and Sandie, she was earning a fair amount from live performances and put this to good use, buying her parents a home in Glasgow's Meadowpark Street, not far from their current address but in terms of opulence and living standards, a world away. For herself she bought a house in St John's Wood which had belonged to Marian Massey's sister. Led Zeppelin's bassist, John Paul Jones, was a neighbour.

In 1966, Lulu's commercial value slumped to an extent that her records made no impression on the singles or album charts, though not on account of mediocre material. Through no fault of her own, the blame for this lack of sales lay squarely at Decca's door for releasing so many duds—a situation which would not improve over the coming years—and for the lack of adequate promotion. Her first single of the year, "Call Me", had been written by Tony Hatch and Jackie Trent for Petula Clark, whose own take, released on a EP, also bombed. The song has since become a classic—the best-known versions at the time were by Chris Montez and Peggy Lee. Lulu does not sing the number particularly well, though by way of contrast the flipside, "After You", is as good as it gets. The English language version of Marie Laforet's French hit, "Apres toi qui sait", it had been earmarked for Cilla, who would have excelled with it. Lulu's voice was frequently too strident for ballads. Maybe had she exercised a little more restraint in her upper register, instead of going in for over-embellishment, she would have mastered the art of performing this kind of material. Joss Basselli, who wrote the original for Marie Laforet, told me that he had done his utmost to *prevent* Lulu from covering it—even going so far as to put an embargo on her using Laforet's English lyrics, which she had recorded two years earlier. Decca merely commissioned new ones, and in Lulu's favour it has to be said that she performs the piece exceptionally well.

Lulu's contract with Decca expired in March 1966, when she signed a deal with Columbia—the company which had rejected her two years earlier—

and Epic in the United States. One Decca single was left in the can: ex-Animal Alan Price's "Oh What A Wonderful Feeling", released in the September, was supposed to be a duet, though Price's contribution is no more than that of a backing singer. Lulu's first release for Columbia, in March 1967, was a cover of Neil Diamond's "The Boat That I Row". It was her best in a while, reaching Number 6 in the charts —one place higher than "Shout". All that was left for Decca to do as part of their deal was release an album, *Lulu*, on their budget Ace Of Clubs label. This was a compilation of A and B-sides supplemented by five unremarkable new songs.

Marvin Gaye had written "Stubborn Kinda Fellow" in 1962: the lyrics describe his erratic behaviour while married to Anna, sister of Motown founder Berry Gordy. Why Lulu wanted to cover this is baffling. "Lies", written by Buddy Randell and Beau Charles of The Knickerbockers, was this group's "piss-take" on the Beatles—their attempt to prove that anyone could come up with the Mersey Sound if they tried. Their single reached Number 20 in the US charts, and many hearing it for the first time were convinced that they were listening to the real Fab Four. Lulu makes a mess of it and similarly ruins Liverpool songwriter Tony Hazzard's "Bye Bye Heart". Carolyn Varga's "When He Touches Me" is no better, while attempting Cilla's "Don't Answer Me", sees Lulu treading on thin ice. She exonerates herself well during the first few bars, but when she reaches the crescendo she appears to purposely crack her notes, her only way of coping with a dubious upper register which has her ruining the song completely.

Meanwhile, Lulu was contacted by writer-director James Clavell, casting for the film adaptation of E R Braithwaite's autobiographical novel, *To Sir With Love*. The Guyanese-born author had worked as a teacher at a tough East End of London school, suffering racial prejudice from the predominantly white pupils, mostly from broken homes. In the film, Braithwaite becomes Mark Thackeray and Clavell, whose screenwriting credits included *The Great Escape*, had signed black actor Sidney Poitier for the role: in 1955, he had appeared in what is generally regarded as the first film of this genre, *The Blackboard Jungle*, and received universal praise. Though the script was not faithful to the book—its profanities (aside from "bleedin'") would not have got past a 1960s censor—it was hard hitting. The pupils are a nasty bunch, so much so that their last teacher suffered a breakdown and resigned. They are led by Judy Geeson and Christian Roberts, while Lulu plays Barbara Pegg. Thackeray, however, is made of stronger stuff than his predecessor, refuses to capitulate, and in the end wins his pupils' respect.

Some sources state that Clavell specifically requested Lulu for the film, others that Marian Massey approached him first—that to her way of thinking, if Marianne Faithfull was acting on the stage and making films, why should Lulu not do the same, and not with puerile pop nonsense like *Gonks Go Home*? Despite her lack or training, she handled her part admirably, and tackled the gritty dialogue just as well as her more experienced co-stars, some of whom initially resented her because she was the only member of the cast not to have attended drama

225

school. During rehearsals there was a run-in between Lulu and Clavell when he demanded that she change the colour of her hair—bringing the tarty response from her that he should accept her as she was, or not at all. Clavell was so impressed by her fiery no-nonsense mien that, as shooting progressed, her part increased in size.

In 1996, two years after Clavell's death, Peter Bogdanovich would produce a made-for-television sequel with Lulu, Judy Geeson and Sidney Poitier reprising their roles: this saw Mark Thackeray (69-year-old Poitier) emerging from retirement to take up a similar teaching post in Chicago, when his problem pupils this time around were from the city's Hispanic community. Times had however changed: compared to the original film, the sequel was poor and nowhere near as well received.

Lulu's contract stipulated that she perform the film's theme-song, though this was yet to be written when shooting began. James Clavell contacted several well-known songwriters, every one of whom refused the commission: some disliked him—others are thought to have been unhappy with Lulu interpreting their work on account of her poor track record so far as the charts were concerned. The problem was solved by Marian Massey, who had recently taken a young Canadian singer-songwriter named Mark London under her wing—he would subsequently become Massey's second husband.

Mark London's "Stop Fooling Around" had appeared on the flipside of Lulu's "Tell Me Like It Is", and he later produced many of her songs and albums. According to Lulu, he composed the melody of "To Sir With Love" in thirty minutes flat, and Don Black—Matt Monro's manager and the adapter-composer of several of his hits—just as quickly came up with the lyrics which aptly describe the dilemma faced by the pupil who has fallen in love with her teacher, and who may openly admit to this now that she has left school. "How do you thank someone who had taken you from crayons to perfume?" she asks, before deciding that the perfect gift to give him will be her heart. It is a stunning song, perfectly put across and ably backed by Wayne Fontana's group, The Mindbenders, who also appear in the film.

"To Sir With Love" was one of the first songs Lulu recorded as part of a new deal with Columbia, though for some obscure reason the record company did not consider it worthy of the A-side. This honour went to Paul Evans' "Let's Pretend", and the single reached Number 11 in the UK charts—lower than it should have done because of this, some critics maintained. The other number from the film, "Stealing My Love From Me", would for many years be confined to the soundtrack album.

Lulu had a new producer, one of the most egocentric in the business. Aldershot-born Mickie Most (1938-2003) had a varied career. After working as a waiter at Soho's The 2i's Coffee Bar, he formed the short-lived Most Brothers with Alex Wharton—they had a minor hit, "Takes A Whole Lotta Loving To Make My Baby Happy". After disbanding in 1959, Most relocated to South Africa where he formed Mickie Most & The Playboys, a successful outfit which enjoyed eleven successive chart-toppers there. In 1962 he returned to London to work for Columbia. His success stories included

The Animals' "House Of The Rising Sun"—which earned him a Grammy—and hits for Brenda Lee, Herman's Hermits, Donovan—and Lulu, whose seven Most-produced singles all reached the UK Top 50 during the two years they worked together.

Between completing *To Sir With Love* and its release, Lulu taped her first television series. *Three Of A Kind*, scripted by Brad Ashton and Peter Robinson, was a high-camp sitcom co-starring impressionist Mike Yarwood and comedian Sid Fell. The first six episodes, broadcast between June-July 1967, received such good ratings that five more were commissioned and broadcast at the end of the year. Like Cilla, Lulu was possessed of an innate albeit giddy comic timing and would excel in this medium once her recording career slowed down.

To Sir With Love was an unprecedented smash in America, where it premiered in June (three months before Britain, where it was only mildly successful), breaking all the box-office records so far that year. Even so, it took the single—Lulu had recorded the song with a new orchestration and additional lyrics —three months to have any impact on the US charts, by which time she had been lined up with any number of projects. These involved promoting her next UK single, "Love Loves To Love Love", a repetitive piece which stalled at Number 32 in the charts. The B-side, Mark London's "You And I", with its Eastern flavour introduction until the big band sound kicks in, was far superior—a difficult song which Lulu handles with comparative ease, proving that she could hit the high notes if she wanted to, without losing control. As with "To Sir With Love", had the sides been swapped around, the record might have fared better.

Then news came in that "To Sir With Love" had ousted The Box Tops' "The Letter" from the top of the *Billboard* chart, where it would remain for five weeks—Lulu being the only 1960s Brit Girl to achieve this. Suddenly, the Columbia publicity machine went into overdrive as Marian Massey received offers for Lulu to tour all over North America: chat and music shows, concerts, opening shopping malls, the works. Massey turned most of them down. Lulu had a full diary of commitments at home, and it was only fair that these should take precedence. To her way of thinking Blackpool and Leeds were no less important than Las Vegas and Los Angeles, if these had booked her first.

Massey compromised by organising a "super-lightning" if not exhausting trip across the Atlantic. On 22 October, Lulu flew to New York where a press-conference took place at the airport, followed by another at the Drake Hotel. She was then driven to the studios for a last-minute appearance on Ed Sullivan's *Talk Of The Town*, where in a black dress with white lace edgings she sang "To Sir With Love" before being whisked back to the hotel. The next morning she boarded the plane back to London for rehearsals for her spot on the Royal Variety Show. Also appearing on the bill this year were Sandie Shaw, Tom Jones, and Vikki Carr.

Lulu's second album of 1967, *Love Loves To Love Lulu*, was again poor value for money so far as the fans were concerned, and did not chart. Running at just 32 minutes, five of the eleven tracks had been previously released as A and B-sides, and what remained was far from exceptional. "Morning Dew" was a 1962 folk song from Canadian vocalist Bonnie Dobson—inspired by the film, *On The Beach*. Lulu's version, despite her tendency to go a little haywire in the upper register, is performed with feeling and superior to the better-known reading by Ralph McTell. "Rattler", her venture into country and western, is *so* good that one momentarily forgets that Lulu was only nineteen when she recorded it. Bruce Woodley of The Seekers—Cilla had done a great job with his "Red Rubber Ball"—had written this road-song shortly before the Australian group's split. The "rattler" in the title was not—as many Americans believed—a snake, but the cronky train taking the singer home to her lover after a lengthy separation. The Bee Gees' "To Love Somebody" had been written for Otis Redding, who had not lived to record it. Many artistes had covered it, most notably The Flying Burrito Brothers. The orchestration is superb, and for once Mickie Most does not rush for the fade button. Finally there was "Take Me In Your Arms And Love Me", a 1967 UK hit for Gladys Knight & The Pips.

Soon after completing the album, Lulu returned to America, this time for a more leisurely visit. She was handled Stateside by Sandy Gallen, renowned as a member of the all-powerful political media group, "The Velvet Mafia"—subsequently renamed "The Gay Mafia" when this word came into more common usage—whose other members included Truman Capote, Andy Warhol, and Calvin Klein. Later, Gallen would manage Michael Jackson and Dolly Parton. Over the course of the next two weeks Lulu guested on Johnny Carson's *Tonight*, and *The*

Joey Bishop Show. She and Bishop, a member of Frank Sinatra's infamous Brat Pack, had a friendly altercation on live television when he introduced her as an English singer. In her broadest Glaswegian, Lulu "sternly" admonished, "Ah'm not English, ah'm Scottish!" The audience, thinking it part of the repartee, howled with laughter. She also appeared on *The David Frost Show* with Laurence Olivier and Peter Sellers. Her admission, however, that she had literally stopped the traffic while strolling through New York was only partly true. Sandy Gallen's assistant is believed to have walked ahead of her to inform taxi drivers who she was so that they could shout at her and blow their horns. And of course, there just happened to be a photographer close at hand to snap her chatting to these "fans" who otherwise might not have recognised her in the crowded street.

Though she was not exactly "America's favourite sweetheart", as she also claimed, Lulu was given the opportunity to make it even bigger in America, courtesy of Sandy Gallen, who on the strength of her appearance on *The Joey Bishop Show* negotiated a five-year contract said to be in the region of $2 million. All she had to do was relocate to New York or Los Angeles. The offer was turned down not by her but by Marian Massey, who allegedly did not wish to lose out by allowing the act *she* had launched and nurtured to earn commission for someone else. As such, like most of the other Brit Girls, Lulu stayed where many believed she belonged—with the Brits!

231

Lulu & The Luvvers, 1965.

In *To Sir With Love* (1967)

3: Boom-Bang-A-Bang!

Early in 1968, Lulu began working on her first television series proper—a variety show, as opposed to a sitcom. Between now and 1975 she would enjoy success on the small screen with *Lulu's Back In Town, It's Happening For Lulu, Lulu,* and *It's Lulu!*, where her regular guest was Adrienne Posta. Another regular was Dudley Moore, who developed his infamous (with Peter Cook) Derek and Clive routine during breaks from filming, using Lulu as a sounding board for his copiously vulgar sketches. Over the years other guests included home-grown talents Les Dawson and Malcolm Roberts, and international stars such as the Everly Brothers and Jimi Hendrix. The Wild Man Of Rock's appearance on the live 4 January 1970 edition of *It's Happening For Lulu* made headlines when, having paid tribute to Cream, whose split had been announced that day, he refused to leave the stage after performing his contracted solo spot. When prompted by one of the technicians to exit the set so that Lulu could perform her closing number before the titles went up, Hendrix let rip with a growled, "Fuuuuuck you!" The outburst saw him banned from ever appearing on the BBC again.

For a while, there would be no return to the big screen, though it would appear not through any lack of trying on a certain mysterious producer's part. In her memoirs, Lulu recalls how she was wooed by an Arab film mogul—the only clue to his identity being that he was in his early forties, with slightly greying hair—a lecher who appears to have been less interested in having Lulu play Nerfertiti in one of his productions than he was in getting her into his bed. "Nefertiti! Me!" she writes, "You've got to be kidding. Maybe I could play some rough diamond or urchin, but not a celebrated beauty!" The episode she humorously recalls might have made for an interesting sketch in a sitcom, had it not been for the underlying element of probable danger. The mogul pestered her for days, until Lulu got a male friend to warn him to back off.

Compared to most of her contemporaries, Lulu's love-life appears to have been uncomplicated. Sex, she said her mother had told her one assumes speaking from personal experience, was something which men enjoyed and women forced themselves to put up with. Like Cilla, and like any other well-raised girl of her generation, she had strong moral values and adhered to the sex-follows-marriage-follows-courting rules of the day. In the pop world, however, and most especially at the height of the Swinging Sixties, chastity was not always a quality to boast about when invited to parties, where *not* seen to be pairing off was frequently considered anti-social. Lulu speaks of her "innocent romances", the crushes she had on Scott Walker, Peter Noone of Herman's Hermits, Eric Clapton, and footballer George Best—though her biggest fascination was for 21-year-old Davy Jones (1945-2012), the pint-sized vocalist with The Monkees, with whom she toured in the summer of 1967.

The Monkees had come about the previous year when two US producers had auditioned 400 hopefuls to form a group similar to the one in the Beatles' film, *A Hard Days Night*. A clutch of chart-topping albums and singles had followed in rapid succession. Manchester-born Jones, the group's only non-American member, was a stage veteran who had played The Artful Dodger in the London and Broadway productions of Lionel Bart's *Oliver!*, and he had been on the bill when the Beatles debuted on Ed Sullivan's *Talk Of The Town*. Jones may have looked baby-faced and innocent, but he was very much a ladies' man who was clearly expecting more from Lulu than she was willing to give—therefore she was understandably annoyed when her refusal to take this and her other "dalliances" as far as the bedroom was lampooned by celebrity photographer David Bailey, who captioned one magazine picture he had taken of her, "The Virgin Queen Of Pop".

"I hadn't announced my virginity or preached chastity," Lulu said, "I thought I'd done a good job keeping it hidden. Obviously not."

Lulu recalled her reaction to a game of "pass the joint" at one of Brian Epstein's parties, though in the end she did not succumb to temptation: "I didn't want to seem different to everyone else because I wasn't taking drugs....The joint was getting closer. I was terrified of smoking it and equally terrified of being found out."

Meanwhile another man was waiting in the wings. Lulu had known Maurice Gibb for several months, but it was only now that the tabloids began hinting at romance. Born on the Isle of Mann in 1949, he and his family had relocated to Brisbane, Australia, in 1958, and whilst here he had formed The Bee Gees with his twin brother Robin, and their younger brother Barry. A fourth brother, Andy, would have a brief but relatively successful musical career, but tragically succumb to drugs-induced heart disease in 1988, aged just thirty. There was also a non-musical sister, Lesley, the oldest of the siblings. In August 1967 the group had scored their first major UK hit with "New York Mining Disaster" and they later topped the charts with "Massachussets"—attracting praise from some critics, whilst others had mocked Robin Gibb's braying "nanny goat" vocals.

Lulu and Maurice Gibb are thought to have met backstage in the *Top Of The Pops* studio. They had dated briefly, she had not taken the relationship seriously, and he had moved on. In January 1968, when Lulu opened for a week's cabaret at Luton's Caesar' Palace, whilst still obviously worshipping Gibb from afar—the Bee Gees' manager, Robert Stigwood, told one newspaper that her bedroom wall was "plastered with pictures" of him—she took her crush on Davy Jones to the next level.

The tabloids ran stories of a passionate love affair, while Lulu's mother advised her not to marry Jones because, in her opinion, small men were invariably "cursed with Napoleon complexes".

The love affair proved short-lived when The Monkees left for a tour of Germany—ironically with the Bee Gees, so one may only imagine the underlying tension while they were all on the road. Lulu, meanwhile, worked a two-week stint at the Talk Of The Town, after which she picked up a gong at the *Disc & Music Echo* awards for Top Television Personality of the Year. She released a new single: Tony Hazzard's "Me, The Peaceful Heart" reached Number 9 in the charts, despite not being one of the best songs she had recorded in a while. She then flew to Los Angeles to prepare for a sell-out season at the Cocoanut Grove. This saw her arriving in a bad mood, when Davy Jones promised to meet her at the airport, but failed to turn up. This was the first crack in their relationship. Soon she would be denouncing him as surly, bad-tempered and over-possessive. What she did not know was that, probably because *their* affair did not involve the sex which he doubtless wanted, Jones had gone looking for this elsewhere. The woman in question, Linda Haines, was later disclosed as his long-term girlfriend though everyone but Lulu appears to have known this. Not only this, Haines was expecting his baby.

The management of the Cocoanut Grove have maintained that Lulu was edgy during rehearsals, first complaining about the lighting, then about the resident orchestra who had recently accompanied Peggy Lee and Frank Sinatra. There *were* a few hitches on opening night, none of them Lulu's fault, and the evening, along with the entire season, was declared a triumph. As had happened with *The Joey Bishop Show*, the audience roared at her ticking off of the musicians, thinking this part of her act. The *Hollywood Reporter* applauded her "contagious charm", while *Variety* enthused, "Lulu's A Winner!" Each evening, after the show, Davy Jones would be there, apparently with just one thought in mind—getting her into bed once they got back to her hotel.

"Often he wouldn't leave until 4:30 a.m., and then only with a lot of coercion," Lulu said.

A few weeks later she learned of Jones' affair with Linda Haines, and the two-timing singer was given his marching orders.

In May, Columbia released "Boy", a catchy but corny piece written by "Howard Blakely"—aka the team of Ken Howard and Alan Blakely, who penned hits for The Honeycombs, and all fifteen Dave Dee, Dozy, Beaky, Mick & Titch A and B-sides released between 1965 and 1969. The flipside, Mark London's bouncy country-style "Sad Memories", is much better. Clearly, so far as getting it wrong where singles were concerned, Columbia were already travelling down the same road as Decca.

At this time, Lulu was reunited with Maurice Gibb. Absence had certainly made the heart grow fonder, and now she could not wait to tell the world that she was madly in love. At the end of October— the same week that Davy Jones married eight-months pregnant Linda Haines—Gibb asked Lulu to marry him and she accepted. For a while, the news was kept out of the press: the actual announcement was made on television during a live episode of *Happening For Lulu* when Mo, as she always called him, was her special guest. She ended the year by releasing "I'm A Tiger", not one of early-60s rocker Marty Wilde's better compositions, though it reached Number 9 in the charts. Again, the B-side is better: Lulu's version of "Without Him" is perhaps the definitive take of the Harry Nilsson classic—the blending of her voice, restrained in its lower register with the collegiate strings is breathtaking.

In January 1969, Bill Cotton, the BBC's head of light entertainment, chose Lulu to represent the United Kingdom in the Eurovision Song Contest. Many years later she would claim that she had been against the proposition, deeming the voting "too political" and the songs "too ordinary". She was of course speaking as things stood in 2002 when she published her autobiography—when voting *was* politically rigged, and most of the songs performed

238

in English as opposed to the participating countries' native languages.

Backed by the Johnny Harris Orchestra, Lulu sang one of the six shortlisted songs each week on *Happening For Lulu*, then all of them in a special programme hosted by Michael Aspel. "Are You Ready For Love" and "Betcha" were representative of the typical Eurovision fare of the next generation, when standards dropped dramatically, but the other four numbers were rather good.

Howard Blakeley's "March" was almost the kind of boisterous number one imagines being performed in the parade yard in a 1950s military biopic. Mark London's jazzy, Italianate "Come September" may well have been inspired by the Rock Hudson-Gina Lollobrigida movie of the same name. "I Can't Go On Living Without Your Love" was an early collaboration by Elton John and Bernie Taupin. Aspel introduced them as Elton Jones and Bernie Poppins! But, one wonders in retrospect, would it have won the contest? It was Lulu's favourite, but in the voting came last—gaining only 5,000 of the 125,000 public votes. Later, it would be covered by Cilla and Sandie. The song chosen by viewers, gaining 56,000 votes ("March" came second with 38,000) was "Boom Bang-A-Bang", another so-called "farting oompah" piece composed by Alan Moorhouse and Peter Warne—the latter had written "Kiss Me Honey, Honey, Kiss Me" for Shirley Bassey. As had happened with Sandie, the one chosen was the one Lulu liked the least!

In the meantime, on 18 February Lulu and Maurice Gibb were wed at St James' Church, Gerrard's Cross: given away by her father, the bride

239

wore a white, fur-trimmed hooded coat over a short white dress. Barry Gibb was best man, replacing Lulu's brother, Billy, who initially disapproved of the couple tying the knot, declaring them too young—while the page-boys included Andy, the youngest of the Gibb clan. The reception took place at La Gavroche, near Sloan Square, but there was no honeymoon—Lulu was in the middle of filming her latest television series and recording a second album for Mickie Most, and The Bee Gees also had work commitments. The marriage would prove a stormy one. Lulu described them as, "Two spoiled little pop stars, with too much money and not enough sense."

Gibb, it would appear, was a control freak whose personal and professional relationships frequently proved volatile, with Lulu caught in the crossfire. This much she confessed. Home was Woodley, a seven-bedroomed house in Highgate. Ringo and Maureen Starr lived nearby.

Lulu's Album was by far the best thing she did during the Sixties, primarily because *she* chose the material. The production and interpretations were first class, and none of the songs had been previously released on singles. This time the fans were in for a surprising treat—that is, once they had got past Joe Tex's "Show Me", the only track not worthy of comment. Bob Dylan's "The Mighty Quinn" had provided a recent hit for Manfred Mann, but Lulu injects life to this formerly dirge-like piece by giving it a splendid big band arrangement. One wonders if she, with her intolerance towards drugs, ever worked out or was told what some of these "metaphorical" lyrics were about. Dylan claimed that they centered around the

240

Anthony Quinn character in *The Eskimo*, but critics have suggested otherwise, that "Quinn the Eskimo" may have been his nickname of one of his drug dealers.

Wilfrid Mills and Laura Lemon's "My Ain Folk" dates back to 1904, and had featured in the repertoire of one of England's first major recording stars, Dame Clara Butt (1872-1936). The lyrics, which Lulu pronounces clearly and intimately, express the emigrant's longing for her homeland. Lulu regularly performed the song whenever she returned to Glasgow, rarely receiving less than a rapturous welcome and standing ovation where many people still referred to her as Marie Lawrie. After Don Black and Mark London's so-so "Where Did You Come From?" comes Spencer Davis and Steve Winwood's tuneless, ear-splitting "Gimme Some Loving", one of the few duds here. The Bee Gees' "I Started A Joke" had been promoted as "a song about social alienation": the narrator tries everything to make an impression on the world, but is only noticed after he dies. Whereas the group's version droned on—those "nanny-goat" voices again—Lulu gives it some "wallop", making it her own and sending shivers down the spine.

Lulu also triumphs with "Why Did I Choose You?", one of Barbra Streisand's signature songs and arguably the most perfect performance on this overall exquisite album. No less authoritative is her reading of Hugh Martin and Ralph Blane's "The Boy Next Door", which Judy Garland had performed in *Meet Me In St Louis*. And after "Come September" is Bacharach and David's "A House Is Not A Home", a minor hit for Dionne Warwick—as

241

usual Lulu, Dusty and Barbra sang it better. Sadly, the album concludes on a mediocre note with The Box Tops' "Cry Like A Baby".

A smaller delegation accompanied Lulu to Madrid for the Eurovision Song Contest than those that had been organised for Sandie Shaw and Kathy Kirby, Later she boasted that as most of the entrants were unknown outside their respective countries, *they* had nothing to lose and everything to gain by entering the competition: "I was an internationally famous pop star and, consequently, the raging favourite. Anything less than outright victory would have been seen as a failure."

Had she made such a blatantly arrogant remark at the time, she would have been shown no mercy by the Continental media. The actual favourites were France's Frida Boccara and Monaco's 12-year-old singing sensation Jean-Jacques who sang "Maman-Maman". Also, though some of the singers—particularly Boccara—may not have been known in Britain, they sold more records that year in Europe than Lulu would sell in the entire decade.

The contest took place at the city's Téatro Réal on 29 March, and Lulu's backing singers were Sue and Sunny—soon afterwards they joined Brotherhood Of Man, who won the contest in 1976. For the first and last time in the show's history there was more than one winner: Spain's Salome with "Viva Cantando", Holland's Lenny Kuhr with "De troubadour", Frida Boccara with "Un jour un enfant"—and Lulu. In fact, had the current tie-break rule been in force then ("The winner is deemed to be the country receiving the most votes, and if there is a tie, the winner is the country receiving the most high votes.") France would have been declared overall winner. Lulu recorded "Boom Bang-A-Bang" in German, Spanish, Italian and French. The English version reached Number 2 in the charts—her biggest UK hit—but came way behind the Boccara and Jean-Jacques songs in European sales. Indeed, the best-selling Eurovision songs to date have been Boccara's "Un jour un enfant" and Abba's "Waterloo". The first of several Eurovision winners with silly titles, it was also lampooned by the Monty Python team—in their hands it became "Bing-Tiddle-Tiddle-Bong". Equally ridiculously, along with Cher's "Bang-Bang", the song was deemed "insensitive" by the BBC and banned from the airwaves during the Gulf War.

Lulu's bravado on the subject would not diminish, and years later she boasted to John Peel, "I know it's a rotten song, but I won, so who cares? I'd have sung Baa Baa Black Sheep standing on my head if that's what it took to win....I'm just so glad I didn't finish second like all the other Brits before me!"

She was referring to Kathy Kirby, and to Cliff Richard's losing the contest (also held in Madrid the previous year) by just one vote—allegedly because of vote-rigging on behalf of the Franco dictatorship. Today, she never misses out on an opportunity to get this point across.

In the wake of Eurovision, Lulu's international career could have reached unprecedented heights. Sadly, she rejected more offers than she should have done because she did not want to be separated from her husband for lengthy periods. As had happened with Marianne Faithfull and Mick Jagger at the height of their romance, his career took precedence

243

over hers, almost certainly a guaranteed recipe for disaster. The couple flew to the West Indies, then to Mexico, for a belated honeymoon. Upon her return to Britain she decided that she needed to be performing songs more suited to her torchy voice than some of the "rinky-dink and lightweight" ones which Mickie Most had been fixing her up with. She was right: the sheer quality of the material on *Lulu's Album* was testament to this. Therefore when her contract with Most expired, she elected not to renew it. Several numbers which Most had arranged for her to record were given to other artistes, including Nancy Sinatra, who had a minor hit with "The Highway Song".

At around this time Lulu appeared in *Cucumber Castle*, a television special devised by Maurice and Barry Gibb with a plot which may only be dismissed as too daft to laugh at: two medieval brothers inherit their father's realm, Cucumber Kingdom, and become involved in a series of dopey adventures with Pat Coombes, Eric Clapton and Spike Milligan, while singing a clutch of Bee Gees songs. Lulu was their damsel in distress.

Almost certainly Lulu's dropping of Mickie Most, while at the zenith of her popularity, had been Maurice Gibb's idea. And now, her controlling husband suggested that she might be better off transferring her talents Stateside...

With Davey Jones.

With Jimi Hendrix during rehearsals for her
television show.

With first husband Maurice Gibb.

After Eurovision!

3: Best Of Both Worlds

By following in Dusty's footsteps and allowing herself to be taken under Jerry Wexler's wing, Lulu was taking a step in the right direction. Of all the Brit Girls, *only* she and Dusty had the voice suited to being produced by such a man. She did not sign with Atlantic Records but with their subsidiary label, Atco, and unlike Dusty did not allow herself to be manipulated. She knew exactly what she wanted to sing, as opposed to being told *what* to perform, though she did agree to consider Wexler's choices first. Her mother (who had recently shocked the Lawrie clan by becoming a Mormon) accompanied her to Miami where without ceremony or an attendant press-attaché they were met by Wexler, and driven from the airport directly to the studio, where she was introduced to his partners, Tom Dowd and Arif Mardin. Here, she was pleased to learn that Wexler had more or less chosen the songs she would have selected herself: his working relationship with Lulu would prove much less fraught than the one with Dusty.

Over the next few weeks, a number of tracks were put down at the Mussel Shoals Studio, Alabama, resulting in the album, *New Routes*, which many consider almost on a par with *Dusty In Memphis*. Her musicians included ace guitarist Duane Allman, and Eddie Hinton—the studio's resident guitarist who had worked with Elvis Presley and Aretha Franklin. Dusty had covered his "Breakfast In Bed", and Lulu now recorded his "Where's Eddie?" Other excellent tracks included "In The Morning", the Bee Gees' "Marley", and a fine version of Jerry Jeff Walker's "Mr Bojangles". The following year, Lulu recorded *Melody Fair*, title courtesy of another Gibb brothers collaboration. This included their "In The Morning Of My Life", though it was Andy Gibb's and later Nina Simone' versions of the song which would be best remembered. Both albums did well in America and a single from *New Routes*, "Oh Me Oh My" reached Number 22 on the *Billboard* chart. In Britain they bombed. Equally unsuccessful —but not lacking in quality—were four original songs which Lulu recorded for the German market: these were released on the EP, *Traurig Aber Wahr*.

Working in America and promoting the new albums heralded the demise of Lulu's already shaky marriage as the enforced separations from Maurice Gibb grew lengthier. Occasionally she would fly back to London, where he was appearing on the West End stage with Barbara Windsor in *Sing A Rude Song*, a revue based on the life of music-hall star Marie Lloyd. Lulu would blame the failure of her marriage on Gibb's drinking, his fondness for telling "tall tales", and their immaturity. They were, she said, not sufficiently grown up to start the family she clearly wanted, as they were far too busy living life in the fast lane, spending vast amounts on cars, jewellery, overseas trips, and entertaining their friends. Yet neither could be described as selfish, even though she may have thought this: for years she had been supporting her family, buying her parents one apartment or house after another until she eventually brought them down to London where they could be close to her now that they were getting older. Likewise Gibb had taken her brother Billy under his wing, entering into a business venture with him.

Lulu appears to have tried her utmost to save her marriage, consulting a counsellor, pressurising Gibb to do the same. She claimed that the stress made her physically ill, but the underlying problem seems to have been her fears that, like her parents, she and Gibb would end up staying together only for the sake of it and that their children, if they had any, would suffer unduly the way she and her siblings had done. The crunch came when she was asked to participate in the Hong Kong Arts Festival. The Bee Gees were about to embark on an American tour, and it was mutually agreed that when Lulu returned home, Gibb would have moved out of her house. This way, she hoped, the split would be kept out of the press until they had put together an official statement. Unfortunately, Gibb went back on his word. "I should have loved us to have had a baby, but she was working all the time," he told journalists at Heathrow, implying that this, as opposed to his reputed unsocial habits, was the real reason for their separation.

In May 1972, Lulu was Eamon Andrews' "victim" foe *This Is Your Life*, an experience she did not enjoy—and a ridiculous one, bearing in mind that her life thus far had only taken up twenty-three years. Andrews nabbed her during rehearsals for her television show. Her entire family were gathered in the studio, and there was a filmed message from Sidney Poitier who it was said had already forgotten her. *She* had certainly forgotten most of the other guests who turned up to pay tribute to her.

She recalled, "Eamonn would say, 'Do you remember this voice?' And I'd think, Not a bloody clue."

249

That year she followed in the footsteps of Margaret Lockwood, Wendy Craig, Maggie Smith, and a host of famous actresses when she appeared in *Peter Pan*, at Manchester's Palace Theatre—not the pantomime, but the play staged annually since premiering in 1904, the exception being the first two years of World War II. The run was a success, breaking box office records held since 1934. Lulu would reprise the role several times, including a musical version at the London Palladium in 1975, when Ron Moody played Captain Hook.

Lulu also had a new man in her life. John Frieda, three years her junior, was a hair stylist with her regular salon, Leonards of Mayfair. Quiet and unassuming, and a descendant of Polish Jews who had settled in England at the turn of the century, Frieda was the opposite of the flamboyant Maurice Gibb. The couple succeeded in keeping their romance under wraps until exposed by the tabloids in 1974. Indeed, Lulu frequently denied they were an item, telling journalists he was a friend of her brother Billy. Some critics were unnecessarily hard on her, particularly the *Daily Express'* acid-tongued Jean Rook, who treated almost everyone with the same disrespect. Even Lulu's family believed that her standards had dropped—from a Bee Gee to a "lowly crimper". Yet many legendary stars had ended up in long-term relationships with or married their hairdressers—notably Barbara Streisand (Jon Peters) and Edith Piaf (Théo Sarapo).

Being with Frieda did little to prevent Lulu from having an affair with David Bowie, whom she had known for a while and of whom she recalled, "He had beautiful thighs, the best I've ever seen."

250

The pair bumped into one another in Sheffield, in the autumn of 1973, when he was on tour and Lulu appearing at the city's Fiesta nightclub. Bowie now suggested they work together, and her comeback of sorts (though truthfully she had never been away) took place early the next year when she released a cover version of his "The Man Who Saved The World", c/w "Watch That Man". Bowie himself produced, providing saxophone and (along with Billy Lawrie) backing vocals. Lulu promoted the single on *Top Of The Pops*, dressed as a gangster. The record reached Number 3 in the charts.

More successes with Bowie could have followed. An album is believed to have been discussed, but Lulu opted to put some distance between them, she said, because he was married (to Angie) and his blend of hedonism and decadence was not for her: "He lived on the very edge—sometimes not eating or sleeping for days at a time, experimenting with anything and everything."

Lulu was offended by Bowie's quip, coming from a man whose bisexuality was legendary, made after hearing her speaking on the phone to John Frieda, "Hairdressers are all poofs!"

Therefore it was back to a more stable relationship with Frieda, now that she had had her fun and her marriage to Maurice Gibb was well and truly over, though Frieda was accused in some circles of being a gold-digger. This was untrue, though on account of his involvement with Lulu his list of celebrity clients had increased considerably. He had recently opened his own salon, the first of several.

That same year, Lulu performed the title-song for the Bond film, *The Man With The Golden Gun*, one of the few James Bond themes not to chart. She appeared in her first serious film since *To Sir With Love*, though *The Cherry Picker*, directed by Peter Curran—best known for the *Captain Scarlet & The Mysterons* television series—could hardly be classed as ground-breaking cinema and proved a thorough waste of her, Spike Milligan and Wilfrid Hyde White's talents. The silly story told of a VIP's drop-out son (Bob Sherman) who organises a sleep-in at Windsor Castle. Lulu's character, Nancy, is dispatched to oust him—how, why and what happens next is unimportant—and save him from suicide. In the course of the ensuing scenario she submits to a sex scene—mild stuff compared to today—though Lulu made a fuss about this at the time. Such was her opinion of the film that in her memoirs she observes how the production company ran out of money and could not complete it. This is untrue though it has never been shown on television or released commercially.

On 8 October, Lulu and John Frieda were married at Hampstead Registry Office. As with her first marriage, there was no honeymoon: she was too busy working on her latest television series, and rehearsing for *Aladdin*, scheduled to open in Oxford at the end of the year. She may not have been aware of the fact, but she was several weeks pregnant—her son, Jordan, was born the following June. In her memoirs she writes that she had always wanted four children—that Frieda wanted six—but admits that she had always been the one coming up with the excuse not to have another child "for the time being", until eventually she had left it too late. Jordan attended Eton and Cambridge, and later took up acting. He appeared in Steven Spielberg's television mini-series, *Band Of Brothers*, and in 2002 more controversially played the title-role in the American television movie, *Prince William*— the heir to the British throne had been a fellow student at Eton.

Like the other Brit Girls, changes in musical tastes compelled Lulu to endure her "wilderness" years. Label changes resulted in innumerable single/album releases, not all of them bad despite their failure to chart. Her concert tours and nightclub appearances were no less popular than they had ever been—for a time, her sister Edwina was employed as a backing singer. From the late Sixties until the early Eighties she was the face of the Freeman's fashion catalogue. Later she confessed that she had rarely worn any of their products, and in a way denounced them by adding, "I could afford to buy clothes by the world's top fashion designers. My wardrobe was full of expensive, beautifully tailored clothes that were the cutting edge of fashion."

Lulu became a spokeswoman for the Conservative Party when she augmented Margaret Thatcher's 1979 electoral campaign, and was invited to stand on the Iron Lady's personal platform. This is reputed to have lost her a large number of gay fans when the Thatcher government introduced the hated Section 28 which denounced the acceptance and promotion of homosexuality.

Coinciding with the Thatcher campaign was a summer season in Margate, where Lulu was on her way back to her rented cottage on the outskirts of the town in dense fog, when her car crashed into an oncoming vehicle. Her face smashed into the steering wheel, and she received additional injuries from the shattered windscreen. She was rushed to the nearest hospital, where surgeons operated on her scalp for several hours and told her she had been lucky to survive. It took her two months to recover completely and return to work. The accident left her suffering from depression and mood-swings, though outwardly she remained her usual cheerful self.

The following summer, Lulu cut a new album and filmed another series for the BBC, along with six episodes of *Let's Rock*, a made for American television magazine produced and hosted by Jack Good. The format was similar to that of *Ready, Steady, Go!*—the performers miming to their records while mingling with the audience on the dance-floor. In November she appeared in her second Royal Variety Performance—in the *British Rock & Pop* sequence, she sang the Beatles' "Yesterday". Adam & The Ants were on the bill, and controversially mimed to their latest hit: backstage the two discovered they had been born on the same day, a feat which Ant honoured by inviting her to guest in his promo video for "Ant Rap". She also re-recorded all of her old hits for release on an album, *The Very Best Of Lulu*.

In 1981, Lulu had a US Top Twenty hit with "I Could Never Miss You". Though this spent five months on the *Billboard* chart, it only reached Number 62 in the UK. In 1982, she was shortlisted for the London production of *The Pirates Of Penzance*, and was considered for the role of Miss Adelaide in *Guys And Dolls*. Instead, she replaced Gemma Craven in Lloyd Webber's *Song And Dance* at the Palace Theatre. This had opened in the March with Marti Webb in the *Tell Me On A Sunday* first half: the songs were forgettable but Lulu exonerated herself well as the girl who turns up in New York looking for love, and the reviews were favourable. Four weeks into the run, however, she developed a sore throat—a condition which had rarely affected her in the past and possibly on account of her singing a light mezzo in the show, as opposed to her usual tone. A specialist diagnosed blisters on her vocal cords. Forced to undergo an operation, she was forbidden from speaking for two weeks and there was concern that she might not sing again. At around this time she became involved with Eastern philosophy and mysticism, and later maintained that Siddha meditation had helped her through one of the greatest crises of her life.

Upon her recovery, Lulu eased herself back into the business with pantomime and television appearances. In 1984 she co-hosted *Some You Win (Some You Lose)* for Granada, with *Carry On* star Kenneth Williams—a chat show with a difference, where the guests were often interviewed in exotic, far-flung locations. Her greatest thrill, she said, was working with Rock Hudson at his Hollywood home the year before he died. Finally, she accepted the role of Miss Adelaide in *Guys And Dolls*, opposite Norman Rossington. This opened in Bristol in March 1985, and toured for three months—100 performances in Manchester, Birmingham and Edinburgh—before transferring to London's Prince Of Wales Theatre in the July. Miss Adelaide was another light mezzo role. Her big number was "A Bushel And A Peck" and this time Lulu experienced

255

no problems with her voice: for the first time in her career she had taken singing lessons to deal with the very different (from pop) world of musical comedy.

In 1986, Lulu re-recorded "Shout" for Jive Records—the sales figures for the remix were for some reason combined with those of the re-released, far better original single, Decca's way of proving that *they* had got there first, and saw her returning to the upper reaches of the charts—Number 6—after an absence of twelve years. Much was expected as a follow-up and once again her record company chose the wrong material, a lamentable version of Millie Small's "My Boy Lollipop" which bombed.

Lulu's and John Frieda's marriage had been deteriorating for some time, reputedly on account of combined work pressures. She claimed that he had always been a "worrier" and that this had on several occasions affected his health, including a lengthy hospitalisation with a perforated ulcer. While Frieda spent much of his time in New York with Jason, who was finishing his schooling there, Lulu tried to cope with her marital problems by throwing herself into her work. She replaced Julie Walters as Pauline Mole, the young hero's overbearing mother—"Hair by Worzel Gummige, wardrobe by Oxfam,"—in the hugely successful television series, *The Growing Pains Of Adrian Mole*. She appeared in the London production of Charles Dickens' *The Mystery Of Edwin Drood*, and played a season in Bournemouth in Michael Barrymore's *All Wight Laughter Show*. In August 1988, while working with the funnyman, she learned that she was pregnant—yet no sooner had she announced the news, and secretly hoped that another child might save her marriage, than the press were reporting she had suffered a miscarriage. In November 1991, the press reported that she had ended her working relationship with Marian Massey after twenty-five years.

In the meantime, Lulu's career suddenly went into overdrive. She, who had never considered writing her own material before, penned "I Don't Want To Fight" with her brother Billy—the lyrics centered around her marriage break-up, but as she did not want to record this herself, it was offered to Sade, a popular chart act of the day. She rejected it, and it was given to Tina Turner, currently co-producing *What's Love Got To Do With It?*, the biopic about her stormy relationship with sadistic husband Ike. The song, which Lulu used as the title for her 2002 autobiography, was a massive hit for Turner on both sides of the Atlantic and saw Lulu nominated for a Grammy and an Ivor Novello Award.

Lulu's comeback was courtesy of "Independence", a dance track released early in 1993 to reputedly celebrate her split from John Frieda—though they would not divorce until two years later. Like Dusty, she found herself promoting it in small venues and gay clubs, performing mostly to audiences who had not been born when she had first arrived on the scene. The single peaked at Number 11 in the charts and its successor, "I'm Back Again"—a duet with American soul singer Bobby Womack, reached Number 27.

It was this record which grabbed the attention of Nigel Martin-Smith, the manager of Take That, the Manchester boy band formed in 1990. Sandie had started the Brit Girls revival trend by working with the Smiths and Dusty had followed suit with the Pet

257

Shop Boys. Now it was Lulu's turn to "play matron" to a bunch of talented youngsters—though in her favour she had the edge over her contemporaries in that, while Dusty and Sandie had been rescued from the commercial wilderness by these enterprises, *she* was currently riding a wave of renewed popularity. Together she and Take That reprised Dan Hartman's 1979 disco hit, "Relight My Fire", and this zoomed to the top of the UK charts in October 1993, giving the group what would be the second of eleven Number Ones. It provided the perfect ending for what had started out as a tragic year. In January, Lulu had been devastated by news of Maurice Gibb's death. Aged just 53, her former husband had succumbed to volvitis (a twisted intestine) in a Florida clinic. His demise more or less put paid to the Bee Gees, who from now on would perform very rarely.

In 1994, Lulu supported Take That on their world tour. There was speculation in the tabloids that she was amorously involved with 23-year-old Jason Orange, twenty-two years her junior. In her memoirs, she reveals that Orange flirted with her all the time while they were on the road, but that regrettably nothing had happened between them.

"It was a tonic and a distraction and a huge boost to my ego," she wrote of the attention he lavished upon her, "When I'm seventy I'll look back and say, 'Why the hell didn't I sleep with him?'"

As with David Bowie, Lulu's collaboration with Take That was a one-off, and after the tour she again turned her attention to television. Like Marianne, she appeared in two episodes of *Absolutely Fabulous* and later appeared with French

258

& Saunders in a spoof of *Pulp Fiction*, where she played the Uma Thurman character to their Samuel Jackson and John Travolta. In 1997, the trio teamed up for Comic Relief, this time with Kathy Burke and Llewella Gideon as The Sugar Lumps—their send-up of the Spice Girls. Lulu was Baby Spice.

In 1999 Lulu recorded an album, *Where The Poor Boys Dance*. Much was expected of this when the project was assigned to her friend Elton John's Rocket label. Soon afterwards, Rocket was taken over by Mercury, and without Elton's influence the first single from it barely made the lower reaches of the charts. Though the title-track single peaked at Number 24, Mercury shelved the album's release. That same year she teamed up with a British pop star named Kavana. The pair wrote and recorded "Heart Like The Sun", but this was also shelved and would not see the light of day until the release of Kavana's *Best Of....* album in 2007. *Red Alert*, a National Lottery game show, saw Lulu returning to mainstream television as a family entertainer at the end of 1999. She jetted off to America to interview celebrities as had happened with *Some You Win* but, lacking the appeal of the former show, is was soon dropped from the BBC's schedule. It was however not all doom and gloom for Lulu, who at around this time was awarded an OBE by the Queen—whence she became officially known as Lulu Kennedy-Cairns, subsequently revealed to have been her mother's pre-adoption name.

To date, Lulu has not married again, though her name has been romantically linked with several personalities. There was a much-publicised affair with actor Angus MacFadyen—"It was the best sex

I'd ever had. My God, he relit my fire!" she wrote in her memoirs. There was also a relationship with the much younger, famously hirsute soap-star, Stuart Manning.

Lulu still performs regularly today. Her tours see her playing to packed houses everywhere and her records—old and new—continue to sell *and* chart, a privilege not always enjoyed by her Brit Girl contemporaries.

With second husband John Frieda, on their wedding day.

Lulu: 1960s Vinyl Discography

Items marked * with The Luvvers

1964

Shout*/ Forget Me Baby* (Decca F11884)

Can't Hear You No More*/ I Am In Love* (Decca F11965)

Heatwave: Heatwave; What's Easy For Two Is So Hard For One: Nothing Left To Do But Cry; The Trouble With Boys (EP) Decca DFE 8597

Here Comes The Night*/ That's Really Some Good* (Decca F122017)

1965

Satisfied*/ Surprise, Surprise* (Decca F12128)

Leave A Little Love*/ He Don't Want Your Love Anymore* (Decca F12169)

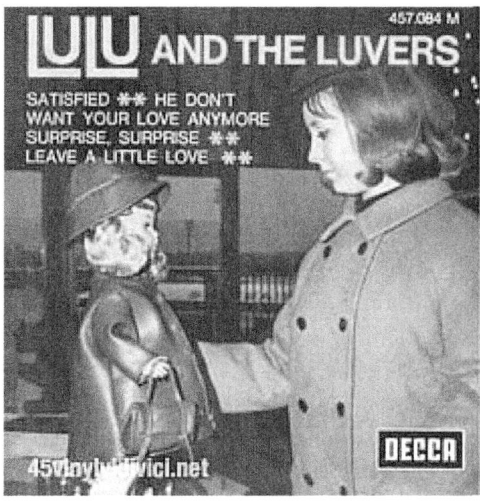

Lulu And The Luvvers: Shout; Forget Me Baby; Can't Hear You No More; I am In Love (EP) Decca 457.085 (France only)

Try To Understand/ Not In This Whole World (Decca F12214)

Something To Shout About: You Touch Me Baby; You'll Never Leave Her; I'll Come Running Over; She Will Break Your Heart; Can I Get A Witness; Tell Me Like It Is; Shout*; Try To Understand; Night Time Is The Right Time; Chocolate Ice*; So In Love; The Only One*; He's Sure The Boy I Love; Leave A Little Love* (Album) Decca LK 4719

That's Really Some Good; Here Comes The Night; Heatwave; What's Easy For Two Is So Hard For One (EP) Decca 457.052 (France only)

Tell Me Like It Is/ Stop Fooling Around (Decca F12254)

*Lulu And The Luvers**: Satisfied; He Don't Want Your Love Anymore; Surprise, Surprise; Leave A Little Love (EP) Decca 457.084. The group's name was misspelt on the sleeve.

1966
Wenn du da bist/ So fing es an
Decca D19760 (Germany only) Sung in German.

Call Me/ After You (Decca F12326)

262

Chocolate Ice; Not In This Whole World; So In Love; He's Sure The Boy I Love (EP) Decca 457.099 (France only)

What A Wonderful Feeling/ Tossin' And Turnin' (Decca F12491)

What A Wonderful Feeling; Tossin' And Turnin'; You Touch Me Baby; You'll Never Leave Her (EP) Decca 457.132 (France only)

1967
Lulu!: Try To Understand; Leave A Little Love; Surprise, Surprise; Stubborn Kinda Fellow; Tossin' And Turnin'; Call Me; Take Me As I Am; Lies; Bye Bye Heart; I'll Come Running Over; Don't Answer Me; Shout (Album) Ace Of Clubs ACL 1232

The Boat That I Row/ Dreary Days And Nights. Columbia CF110 (France only)

263

The Boat That I Row/ Dreary Days And Nights (Columbia DB8169)

Let's Pretend/ To Sir With Love (Columbia DB8221)

Love Loves To Love Lulu: To Sir With Love; Morning Dew; You And I; Rattler; Day Tripper; Love Loves To Love Love; To Love Somebody; The Boat That I Row; Let's Pretend; Take Me In Your Arms And Love Me; Best Of Both Worlds (Album) Columbia SX 6201

Love Loves To Love Love/ You And I (Columbia DB8225)

Best Of Both Worlds/ Love Loves To Love Love Columbia CF127 (France only)

To Sir With Love; Let's Pretend Columbia CF116 (France only)

Lulu Sings To Sir With Love: To Sir With Love; The Boat That I Row; Rattler; Morning Dew; Love Loves To Love Love; Best Of Both Worlds; Day Tripper; Let's Pretend; Take Me In Your Arms And Love Me; To Love Somebody; You And I (album) Epic BN 26339 (USA only)

1968
Me The Peaceful Heart/ Lookout (Columbia DB8358)

Morning Dew/ Rattler Columbia CF133 (France)

264

From Lulu With Love: Here Comes The Night; When He Touches Me; I'll Come Running; Call Me; Surprise, Surprise; Leave A Little Love; Shout; She Will Break Your Heart; Lies; Take Me As I Am; Tell Me Like It Is (album) Parrot PAS 71016. USA only.

Me The Peaceful Heart; Lookout Columbia CF145 (France only)

Boy/ Sad Memories (Columbia DB8425)

I'm A Tiger/ Without Him (Columbia DB8500)

I'm A Tiger/ Without Him Columbia CF180 (France only)

It's Lulu: Show Me; The Mighty Quinn; My Ain Folk; Where Did You Come From; Give Me Some Lovin'; I Started A Joke; Why Did I Choose You; The Boy Next Door; Come September; A House Is Not A Home (album) Epic BN 26536 (USA only)

1969

The World Of Lulu: Leave A Little Love; Don't Answer Me; Surprise, Surprise; When He Touches Me: Call Me; I'll Come Running Over; Shout; Here Comes The Night; Lies; Tell Me Like It Is; Tossin' And Turnin'; Try To Understand (Album) Decca PA 094

Boom Bang-A-Bang/ March (Columbia DB 8550)

Boom Bang-A-Bang (sung in French)/ March Columbia 2C006.04053 (France only) There was also a reprint (2C006.04095) with a different sleeve.

Boom Bang-A-Bang (sung in German)/ Come September Columbia 1C 006-04-074 (Germany)

Boom Bang-A-Bang (sung in Italian)/ March Columbia SCMQ 7134 (Italy only)

Boom Bang-A-Bang (sung in Spanish)/ March La Voz De Su Amo 1J 006.04.053 (Spain only) This was also reprinted (VSL 122) with a different cover.

Estay Loco Por Ti Baby/ Oh Me Oh My/ Barre Tu Puerta De Servicio (sung in Spanish) Atlantic H 533 (Spain only)

Lulu's Album: Show Me; The Mighty Quinn; My Ain Folk; Where Did You Come From; Gimme Some Lovin'; I Started A Joke; Why Did I Choose You; The Boy Next Door; Come September; A House Is Not A Home; Cry Like A Baby (Album) Columbia SX 6265

Oh Me Oh My (I'm A Fool For You Baby)/ Sweep Around Your Own Back Door (Atco 226008)

Sweep Around Your Own Back Door/Oh Me Oh My
Atco 103.178 (France only)

New Routes: Marley Purt Drive; In The Morning; People In Love; After All; Feelin' Alright; Dirty Old Man; Oh Me Oh My; Is That You Love; Mr Bojangles; Where's Eddie; Sweep Around Your Own Back Door (Album) Atco 228031

1970 (recorded 1969)
Povera me (Oh Me, Oh My)/ Hum A Song
Sung in Italian

Melody Fair (some songs recorded 1969): Good Day Sunshine; After The Feeling Is Gone; I Don't Care Anymore; Please Stay; Melody Fair; Take Good Care Of Yourself; Vine Street; Move T My Rhythm; To The Other Woman; Hum A Song; Sweet Memories; Saved (album) ATCO 2400017 (USA only)

Selected Bibliography & Primary Sources

Bret, David: Interviews with Marlene Dietrich, Peter Burton, Dorothy Squires, Marian Montgomery, Kris Kirk, Boz Boorer, Alain Whyte, Boz Boorer, Joss Basselli, Mary Whipp.

Bret, David: *Gracie Fields*, Robson Books, 1995

Bret, David: *Morrissey: Scandal & Passion*, Robson Books, 2004

Bret, David: *Trailblazers: Gram Parsons, Nick Drake & Jeff Buckley*, JR Books, 2009.

Cantacazino, Marina: "Sandie Shaw, Living Up To Life", *Your Life*, 2001

Coleman, Ray: *Brian Epstein*, Viking, 1989

Faithfull, Marianne: *Faithfull* (with David Dalton), Michael Joseph, 1994.

Goodman, Chris: "Sandie Shaw: I Was So Naive", *Daily Express,* 2007

Herman, Gary: *Rock & Roll Babylon*, Plexus, 1982

Hodkinson, Mark: *Marianne Faithfull, As Tears Go By*, Omnibus Press, 1991.

Katz, Gary J: *Death By Rock & Roll*, Robson Books, 1995

Kirk, Kris: Interview with Marianne Faithfull: *A Boy Called Mary*, Millivres, 1999.

Levine, Kitt: "Nothing Less Than Sandie Shaw, *Record Collector*, 1994

Martin, George: *All You Need Is Ears*, Macmillan, 1979

Naughton, John: "Who The Hell Does Sandie Shaw Think She Is?", *The Observer*, 1994

Norman, Philip: *The Life & Good Times Of The Rolling Stones*, Hutchinson, 1989

Peschek, David: "Sandie Shaw: Another Comeback? No Thanks!", *Guardian Unlimited,* 2004

Rogan, Johnny: *Starmakers & Svengalis*, Macdonald, 1988

Sanchez, Tony: *Up & Down With The Rolling Stones*, William Morrow, 1979.

Shaw, Sandie: *The World At My Feet*, Harper Collins, 1991

Shaw, Sandie: "Flashback April 1967", *Observer Music Monthly,* 2007

Teeman, Tim: "From Dageham To Dharma", *The Times,* 2007

Various: "Why Sandie Shaw Has The World At Her Feet", *Sunday Post,*   1991

Various: *The History Of Rock*, Orbis, 1982

Wright-Bouvier, Stephen: "Eurovision Song Contest 1967", no other details.

Printed in Great Britain
by Amazon

48829693R00155